AGAINST MACHISMO

AGAINST MACHISMO

Rubem Alves, Leonardo Boff,
Gustavo Gutiérrez, José Míguez Bonino,
Juan Luis Segundo...and Others
Talk about the Struggle of Women

Interviews by
ELSA TAMEZ

ME Y E R
STONE
BOOKS

Translated and edited by John Eagleson

First published in *Teólogos de la liberación hablan sobre la mujer,*
by Editorial DEI, Apartado Postal 390–2070 Sabanilla,
San José, Costa Rica, © 1986 Editorial Departamento Ecuménico de
Investigaciones (DEI)

English translation © 1987 by Meyer•Stone Books

Published in the United States by Meyer•Stone Books,
a division of Meyer, Stone, and Company, Inc.,
714 South Humphrey, Oak Park, IL 60304

Cover design: Terry Dugan Design

Manufactured in the United States of America
91 90 89   5 4 3 2

Meyer•Stone ISBN 0-940989-12-3 (paper)
Meyer•Stone ISBN 0-940989-13-1 (cloth)

Library of Congress Cataloging-in-Publication Data

Teólogos de la liberación hablan sobre la mujer.   English.
   Against machismo.

      Translation of: Teólogos de la liberación hablan
   sobre la mujer.
   1. Women in Christianity — Latin America. 2. Feminism —
   Religious aspects — Christianity. 3. Feminism — Latin
   America.   I. Alves, Rubem A., 1933–   II. Tamez,
   Elsa. III. Title
   HQ1394.T4613   1987   305.4'2'098   87-21981
   ISBN 0-940989-13-1
   ISBN 0-940989-12-3 (pbk.)

Contents

Preface

If Latin American men do not recognize the reality of women's oppression, if they do not admit that they are promoters or accomplices of the ideology of machismo that permeates our culture, if they do not realize how great the riches that are lost to society due to the marginalization of women, if they do not move from theoretical conviction to liberating practice, if they do not join in solidarity with women in their struggle, the path of the feminist movement in Latin America will be longer, the progress slower and often more bitter, with more frustrations than joys.

The same is true with regard to the struggle for liberation of society as a whole: if there is no qualitatively and quantitatively significant presence of women, if the importance of women and their achievements for the liberation process is not appreciated, and if the fulfillment of women is not fostered, the route to the liberation of society will be longer, less complete, and more conflictive.

The struggle of women is not the struggle of women only; it is not just a women's matter. It is a struggle to be undertaken by all of society, because society in all its dimensions — cultural, social, ecclesial — has suffered the negative effects of the oppression of woman. It is true that women as oppressed subjects must blaze their own trails and assert their own rights. But those trails are not only for the passage of women. They are open trails that need the solidarity of men in the struggle for women's liberation, that need men's participation so that they themselves might be liberated from macho ideology. For this there is required a consensus, a dialogue.

The first steps toward such a dialogue, although still quite timid, have recently been taken on our continent. This is especially true within the grassroots movements; because they are concerned in a fundamental way with the liberation of persons and peoples, these movements have discerned the diversity of subjects involved within the movements, their special insights and their particular struggles.

The Latin American theology of liberation is very much in the vanguard of this timid and recent dialogue between men and women. This is noteworthy since theology is a field traditionally dominated by men. This leadership role, of course, is not coincidental: Since Latin American theology is a theology *of liberation* and a theology that allows itself to be challenged by concrete realities, it has opened its doors to Christian women; they in turn have been attracted by the theology.

Thus women are increasingly joining in the theological task, which naturally facilitates the dialogue. Moreover, there are institutions concerned with assisting and encouraging women in this task; among them are the Ecumenical Association of Third World Theologians (EATWOT), which has undertaken a five-year Women and Theology project, and the Programme of Theological Education (PTE) of the World Council of Churches, which includes among its priorities the theological formation of women. A concrete demonstration of their concern is financial support for this book, which is very much appreciated. This book is an example of the dialogue encouraged by women in order to include men in their struggle and thus achieve a more complete liberation of humankind.

In the concrete case of theology we are trying to show the need to broaden the perspective of theological reflection and biblical hermeneutics to include women's viewpoints, thus enriching and humanizing the discourse that arises from practice. For this reason the theologians' action on behalf of women is basic to the opening of their perspective in their theological reflection.

I have included here interviews of fifteen liberation theologians, both Catholic and Protestant. Personally I believe that the value of these interviews is not so much the level of consciousness of women's oppression — be it high or low — that the theologians demonstrate. It is rather the effort they are making to reflect, perhaps for the first time in some cases, from the angle of those discriminated against because of their sex, an angle that is foreign to some but that needs to be appropriated. I am here referring to their sharing of personal experiences and their attempts to do theology from a women's perspective. I will comment further on this in the second part of this volume.

This book represents only the first part of the dialogue. A second volume will include the reaction and commentary of women theologians to these interviews.

I am profoundly grateful for the warm, sincere, and enthusiastic participation of the theologians interviewed here, the sign of a good beginning.

ELSA TAMEZ

September 17, 1986

Part I

INTERVIEWS

Juan Luis Segundo

Petrópolis, Brazil, July 1985

I was at a meeting of theologians and took advantage of the opportunity to interview Juan Luis Segundo. We were in Petrópolis in one of the countless little rooms of the complicated Franciscan friary that reminds me of the monastery in Umberto Eco's The Name of the Rose. I greatly enjoyed the interview, not so much for what he said; I was more interested in Juan Luis himself, especially his eyes that showed the effort he was making to think through a subject that he perhaps had not thought about before, at least with the same intensity.

Elsa: Juan Luis, what do you think about women's liberation from the point of view of the theology of liberation?

Juan Luis: I think that for now it is not such a good idea to ask that question of those who are supposedly the cause of women's oppression. It's not that I don't want to answer it, but at the present moment in the theology of liberation there are women theologians able to respond much better. It is they who should answer: men should not once again be trying to solve another problem. If women were helpless, as used to be the case in theology, for example, it would be appropriate for the male theologians to try to solve the problem. But now women have much more to say, and what they have to say is of the same theological quality as what men have to say; women are defining

3

their own questions and providing their own solutions within the theology of liberation. I know perfectly capable women who belong to the theological current called the theology of liberation, and I think it is more logical for them to answer the question. But I am willing to discuss to what degree male theologians of liberation are sensitive to these issues.

Elsa: That is my intention, but let me add another question: the theology of liberation has been criticized, especially by feminist theologians of the First World, although not only by them, because it does not include women's issues in its theological discourse. Do you agree with this criticism?

Juan Luis: I think not. I understand the question, and I think that it is perhaps a valid criticism, at least in part, in the First World. But in the Third World the fact that these issues do not appear so explicitly in the theology of liberation does not reflect an ignorance of the problem, but rather a recognition by both men and women that the liberation of the society in which we live is a precondition for truly posing the question of the oppression of women within that society. Both men and women within the theology of liberation in the Third World share the priority of liberating society as a whole.

There is a reason for this that I think should be pointed out to women who are struggling for their liberation in the First World. Insofar as their struggle is uncritical of the ideals of First World society, it becomes a struggle for rights equal to those of men, rights that are translated into consumerism, salaries, social privileges. If women are to be equal to men in their salaries, in their consumption, in their rights in a consumer society — in a country where 6 percent of the world's population consumes 45 percent of the planet's resources — the problem of the distribution of the planet's wealth for all humankind will be made all the greater. And what will be the result? Not only problems for all men living outside the rich countries. It causes problems especially for women, for economic crisis in the poor countries claims women as its first victim.

The wonderful things that women want to achieve and that they should achieve, creativity outside the home, for example, become impossible when economic crises afflict the poor countries, because job possibilities are reduced. And since men will do any kind of work, they take jobs from women whose job possibilities are, for societal reasons, more restricted. That this is the way society should be is debatable, but for now it is the case. So the first effect of the social crises imposed by the rich countries on the poor countries is to send the women back home, because there is no paying work for women. Or at least the work available does not pay adequately, which is to make women into slaves.

If women in the rich countries are not critical of the overall system, they do not realize that their struggle for liberation presupposes the slavery of women in poor countries. And the system in question is not only that internal to the rich countries themselves; it also involves their business relationships and other dealings with poor countries.

That's why I think that in poor countries the issue of the liberation of men and women is understood in a more unified way than is the case in rich countries. It is seen as a problem of common liberation that will allow us to address the oppression of women in a realistic way.

Elsa: Let's look now to the church. Women believe that the church is organized vertically, androcentrically. Do you agree with this? Is it possible to think of a change in the church as it now exists?

Juan Luis: I think that these are two separate questions. I don't think that the vertical structure of the church has much to do with male control of the church. The vertical structure is due to a misunderstanding of the function of authority in the church, an authority that is exercised only from the top down, that gives out information without dialogue — information about what we must think, what we should do, in fact, about everything involving faith, dogma, morality, etc.

Of course, some would say that this is simply a male way of exercising authority; I'm not a psychologist able to say if this is the case or not. But as for the problem of male control, it seems to me that the official church, the church structure, is exclusively male. I think that there is an imbalance here that is not only completely unjust, but also greatly damages the church. It deprives the church of a dimension that is complementary in every functioning human society, every human being. There are feminine elements in men and masculine elements in women, but they are always complementary.

Now it seems to me that this male domination is due to a theological error; there are also certain problems that stem from the constitution of society. The theological error is to think that everything Jesus did in his time is normative without modification for all times. The society in which Jesus lived, like the primitive societies that we more or less know about in the Mediterranean area, was much more of a male society than our society today. Women had less say in public affairs and in anything that involved authority on a societal level. In this sense I don't think Jesus changed anything, simply because he didn't face the problem, or he wasn't sensitive to the problem. Just as he was not sensitive to other problems that would emerge later, like nuclear war and many others. To help him spread the Christian message, he used men, the apostles, and for other tasks he made use of, in a certain sense, the generosity of women. It was women who enabled the community of the apostles to live and to do their work, as we see in the Gospels, but women did not do such work directly.

Through lack of imagination or through the desire to exercise a facile authority, with very clear norms, the church believes that whatever Jesus did must be a direct norm, without taking into consideration differences of context. And so it deduces as a dogmatic consequence, which I think is erroneous, that women should not be ordained, or at least they should not be ordained for the apostolate, for the role of the apostles and thus for the roles of authority and service proper to the apostles. For the apostolate involves roles both of authority and of service. I see no theological reason for such a conclusion.

I do believe that it is relatively difficult to decide this question on a worldwide level in a merely abstract way, deciding that women are equal to men, in the abstract. Achieving equality depends on the evolution of a particular society, and I think we must keep this evolution in mind. You should not, up to a point, violate the social system. The church often violates societies by imposing abstract norms. For example, in a society where there is polygamy the church simply requires men who want to be baptized to get rid of all but one wife. But if they do so, the men commit, at least, an act of supreme selfishness and, moreover, demonstrate a lack of love toward their other wives who are deprived of everything and despised by society. All this because the church does not understand the society.

In deciding whether or not women should undertake certain tasks, I think we must keep in mind the different contexts that exist in different human societies, that is, to what point a society allows women to exercise certain functions. For example, there are societies in which the teaching function is proper to the priest. Until that society develops perhaps that function could not be exercised by a woman since women are restricted to certain functions within that society. But I think we must begin somewhere, especially in societies where women already have a place like men in political, professional, and other functions. My personal opinion as a theologian is that in such cases there is no theological reason why women should not be ordained and, therefore, exercise authority. Whether it is women or men exercising the authority, however, it should not be exercised in a merely vertical manner. But this is another problem, although it is quite possible that women can contribute much to improving our approach to the question of the vertical structures of authority.

Elsa: Juan Luis, I want to talk now about hermeneutics. It seems to me that reading the Bible from the perspective of the poor is easier than reading it from a women's perspective. When we read it from the perspective of the poor we find the keys for a liberating reading in the Bible itself. But when we approach the Bible from the perspective of poor women we encounter certain texts that explicitly discriminate against women. You have done a lot of work on the well-known question of the hermeneutic circle. You have spoken of ideological suspicion in our reading of reality. How do we apply the hermeneutical circle where there is ideological suspicion within the text itself. Can you speak about the hermeneutical process in the reading of the Bible from a women's perspective?

Juan Luis: Yes, I think it is possible to do so. In the first place, as I have tried to explain, the hermeneutical circle has a first moment, which is the moment of suspicion of certain cultural forms. Among these is included Sacred Scripture, because it has developed within specific cultures and not out of thin air. These cultural forms are suspected of being at the service of the controlling interests of society. And we certainly have a long history of a culture made, at least in its most specific forms, by men, although women have had an enormous influence on culture. I don't think we can deny women's influence, but it has not been direct in the formulation of certain cultural artifacts like, for example, written texts. These have usually been written by men.

In this sense we can be suspicious, and in fact we can confirm our suspicions. We must begin to suspect in a systematic way that the books made in cultures where men are in control reflect male interests. There may be a feminine influence, but this influence is as it were hidden, oppressed beneath male influence, and is not apparent.

To a certain extent I think that this part of our suspicion is easy to see and easy to achieve. It will not be difficult for women theologians, who perceive much more immediately than male theologians what they need to be suspicious about. And this is logical, because to ask men to be suspicious of their own control is a little... it is usually not done. It can be done, but men are going to discover only half of what women discover.

The problems in the hermeneutical circle arise when we begin to ask questions about that which constitutes the object of our faith, that is, that which we are unable to change in its overall content. We turn our suspicion on the tradition of the faith and ask how we can believe it, after we have discerned the influences of the controlling interests. This is what happens to the whole Bible. Such interests are discovered not only with regard to women; others interests as well are discovered in the books of the Bible. This certainly does not mean that the Bible is discredited. But when we ask questions of the Bible we must remember that the answers must be questioned still further. And I think that the new question is this: If I eliminate from this message the aspects that derive from male domination of women, what do I have to put back? What do I have to supply? That is, how do we complete the message?

Of course we can always solve the problem by rejecting the message. But I don't think that this is a solution in this case or any other, that is, to reject a message that has validity because of a dominating ideological influence. What we must do is purify the message of that ideological influence. But then we have a problem. I think we should proceed by indicating the elements that women, from their own psychological makeup, from their own way of dealing with things, should add to that message in every age. Because we cannot ask the Bible to reflect back to us what we think today. But surely if I ask of the Bible what women of that time thought about a particular question, I would discover many new things in the Bible. And I would be able to read it better, it would be richer, and God would be more present in the message, because the message would be interpreted more correctly.

There is another problem that I think is much more difficult to resolve; in fact I think it is useless to try to do so. And that is to try to change something that was done in another time, putting it into a different language. I think that it is useless because it contradicts our whole way of dealing honestly with history.

An example is to call God by a feminine name when the Bible uses a masculine one. It's not simply a matter of my not realizing the weakness of that scriptural message. I think it is impossible for us to change, for example, the language of Shakespeare from our present vantage point. We should take Shakespeare as he is or leave him. If Shakespeare in his time had absolutely no concern for social justice, so be it, and I will read him knowing that I cannot find in him something that is not there. And I am not going to introduce passages into Shakespeare that make him say things about social justice that he didn't say. Likewise, I think that women's task with respect to the Bible is not to change it but rather to interpret it from a women's point of view. This will complement an exclusively male point of view of the Bible that stems from its having been written by men in situations where men made the decisions. I believe that such a reading will greatly enrich our understanding of the Bible. But I don't think we should change the language, making it say things that we think it should have said and would have said if we had written it. I don't even think that this is enriching from a cultural point of view. The most creative approach is to complement the text. We should not simply reject it and create another in its place. That's what I think.

Elsa: Thank you very much, Juan Luis.

Julio de Santa Ana

San José, Costa Rica, July 1985

My five-year-old son, Tairo, lent us his toy tape recorder. No other was available. And Franz Hinkelammert lent us one of his cassettes with merengue music on it. It was the weekend, and I wasn't prepared for the interview. On the way to one of the offices of DEI, Julio spoke to me about his work and his next book, Pan, vino, y amistad *(Bread, Wine, and Friendship). And I told him some of my ideas about the Song of Songs. During the interview I sensed in Julio a deep sincerity with regard to the question of women. It seemed that he was a little sad. I didn't know why, and I didn't ask. It was about 10:30 in the morning.*

Elsa: Julio, how would you evaluate the progress of women in Latin America?

Julio: One of the most striking things in recent years has been the increasingly important role women have been playing in social struggles. Let me give you some examples.

Eight years ago, four women with fourteen children entered the offices of the newspaper *Presencia* in La Paz, Bolivia, and began a hunger strike. Later they went to visit the archbishop of La Paz. At that time opposition to Banzer's national security military state was only beginning to be organized. With an unprecedented act of courage those women got the process moving. That small group of weak, helpless people—four in-

11

digenous women and fourteen children — was joined by many
others. Within a month more than three thousand people had
joined them. This destabilized the regime, precipitated the fall
of Banzer, and set Bolivia on a tortuous path toward democracy
and liberalization.

Shortly before this I had been in La Paz to participate in
a meeting of the Assembly of Human Rights, which was held,
I would say, more in fear than in hope. We were afraid that
Banzer forces would interrupt the meeting and arrest the par-
ticipants. But those women got things moving. They were
extraordinary catalysts. That's one example.

Let me give you another, even clearer. During the years of
barbaric repression in Argentina, the only ones courageously to
confront the crimes of the military junta were the women in the
Plaza de Mayo. This was an amazing case. Perhaps the War
over the Falkland Islands and the accumulation of horrors committed by the military accelerated the fall of the Argentinian
military dictatorship. But it was those women who persevered
in the struggle during those long, grim years. And it was at the
risk of their own lives: the first president of the group disappeared; she was assassinated.

After the worst was over and we returned to a normal con-
stitutional rule, the temptation was to cover everything over as
if nothing had happened. But the women of the group insisted
that justice be done. And the spirit with which they did this
was not one of vengeance but to purify the country, which for
me is most important.

These are but two examples. I could give others of women's
participation in the struggles of national liberation. In 1972 the
Tupamaros, the underground resistance movement in Uruguay,
published a booklet called *Actas Tupamaras*. The first chapter is
about the participation of women in the struggle for liberation,
and it presents some striking instances. This is new for Latin
America, a phenomenon that signals the emergence from within
the popular movements of a very courageous current, with its
own characteristics, namely, the women's movement.

When women join in the social struggles they are not only looking for greater freedom, greater justice, but also for recognition. And this requires pondering the future of Latin America, recognizing the presence of women, for the years to come. The liberation of women means not only being able to do things that get women out of the home. More than anything else it means the creation of a world of work where women can begin at the same level as men, something we have not achieved in Latin America.

The work situation for women in Latin America is more or less this: there is a group of women who, for a variety of reasons, are very privileged; they are able to enter into the liberal professional work force. They can be doctors, architects, engineers, schoolteachers, or university professors, but their number is quite limited. Most women, however, join the work force as domestics or as unskilled workers. Great opportunities are not offered to them. Then there is a middle group, sales personnel, secretaries, who likewise are not professionally trained.

By the end of this century we have to create 200 million new jobs in Latin America, and most of them will have to be for women. And this requires training, the creation of conditions for women to enter the workplace not as domestics, not as second-class secretaries or salespeople, but simply as workers. I think that's what it means to recognize women's role. This is how women are going to get the space that they need.

One of the things that most concerns me is that at this point in the history of Latin America, when we seem to be moving beyond the national security states and toward a new democratic synthesis, we see very few women in the legislatures, in leadership positions in politics or government. So there is a gap between the role, I would say the decisive role, that women play in certain areas and the positions they are able to take in society. We have to consider this not only for the present but also looking toward the future. We need to create a new society where women are not simply a reserve labor pool that allows some privileged women to pursue careers at the universities, to be liberated from the full-time care of their children, and to lead a social life.

Elsa: I want to ask a question of you as a married theologian, Julio. When you do theology, do you feel that in some way you integrate your family life, your married life, into your theological discourse?

Julio: I think I have been integrating it more in recent years than previously. Throughout this process, which has meant a revolution in the way we do theology, I have been discovering in a progressive way the presence of the other in, I have to say, a painful way. The formation that we receive is bourgeois; we are trained to be macho bourgeois intellectuals. And the intellectual act is a little like... a sexual act. The intellectual task is an organ, it provides enormous pleasure, and in the same way that we enjoy ourselves sexually with a woman, we also enjoy our intellectual work.

Over the last fifteen or twenty years a new way of doing theology has been developing in Latin America in which we have been discovering the poor. We have been challenged by the poor, challenged to work with them from their own perspective. And we have also been discovering the others whom we have always put in second place, women, our spouses, and our children too. I'm excited to say that the important experiences that have transformed my mental outlook in recent years, since about 1968, have been, first, my encounter with the poor in a slum in Montevideo. Second has been my re-encounter with my wife in what I would call very existential circumstances. And third, my great teachers in recent years have been my children. They have been unsettling my worldview. The poor, my wife, and my children have broken apart the world that I was educated in, a macho world, a world of domination.

Even though we might talk about social justice, deep down we can be very authoritarian. And we learn from others when they unsettle us. This doesn't mean I've learned everything I need to learn. But I'm learning, and they're my teachers.

Specifically, in the case of my relationship with my wife, the books I've written over the last seven or eight years have been gone over by her. There are two reasons for this. First there's friendship. If you live with someone the work you do should be shared with that person. But second it's because my wife writes much better than I do. She's a translator by profession and so knows the rules of grammar better than I. I turn to her for help in improving my Spanish. And if she tells me, for example, "This isn't clear," I know I have to get to work on it. This doesn't mean that I always accept what she says. Sometimes I'll answer, "I want that to stay as it is." And she'll insist that I'm not communicating anything, that what I'm trying to say is meaningless, that it is non-sense.

This involves not only her grammatical skills but I think the feminine element as well. Women have a much greater sense than men of the orientation of meaning. Because we have a very good idea of ourselves and at the same time are great dominators, I think that we men often love to stay on the level of ambivalence, of ambiguity. Women are much clearer. And I don't mean that they love to speak univocally. No, women are much more subtle than that. I mean that women are very precise and realize that things are very mixed in life. But they are more realistic than men.

We shouldn't forget that Greek philosophy, an idealist philosophy, is a male chauvinist philosophy. The slaves in the field and the women at home did the work for the philosophers. And we could be continuing a similar arrangement.

In the last three or four years, my relationship with my wife, Violen, has also been decisive. For various reasons she has been trying to follow a process of affirmation of her feminine identity as a subject of work. She went into psychoanalysis, which helped her enormously and also provoked a development of her personality that began to challenge me. And there were certain things that I refused to take into account in my reflection, but that became inescapable. These challenges have to do with my relationship with her, with our functioning together, especially of me with her. And this has recently led me to look more closely at the relationship between depth psychology and theology and to consider liberation as liberation of the body, as the profound liberation of the person. And this has also helped our relationship.

Elsa: What is a woman for you, Julio?

Julio: For me woman is radical otherness, radical challenge, an enigma. It is very difficult to understand how one can approach a woman; the art of seduction is not a repeatable structure. This is especially true if the woman in question is capable, a woman who is re-creating herself, continuously innovating, and that's the kind of woman who is worthwhile, at least for me. So we have to look for ways that allow us to have a valid relationship with this enigma. I don't know if I'm making myself clear. This applies not only to our mother or wife, but I think the same is true for a daughter as well.

The feminine, then, is otherness confronting our search for our own identity. It is a challenge, an enigma, and I would even say that it can be a reason for our being rerouted. That is, as we grow we are formed by certain influences and we more or less follow an ideal self, our superego. We choose our spouse, not only on a conscious level, but also in accord with that set of ideals that makes up our superego. But the companion that we choose is not only that set of elements that conform to our ideal of the superego; she also brings her own elements. And these reroute us away from our superego; and this is good because the most deceptive part of our being is precisely the superego, which is least real. And so when women reroute us away from our path they lead us into new, unforeseen paths, and this is good. I don't know if I'm making myself clear.

Elsa: It seems that psychoanalysis has helped you a lot.

Julio: To talk about these things I think we have to get into depth psychology. I can't resolve my relationships with women simply on a societal level, on the level of social structures. I have to resolve them on a very deep level. The first person I ever knew was a woman, a very complex woman, for all women are complex. She carried not only me in her womb, but before that she had carried my sister. And she had also carried in her womb another person, the creator of my sister and me, that is, my father. So there is a chain, a complexity of loves in this person, which in one way or another I must have resented, and I have to accept this complexity.

I think that men usually want to simplify, to "reify" women and not accept them in their complexity. And if we do accept them in their complexity we are shaken as if by an earthquake, constantly. There is an important element of fear that men feel toward women, woman as the other, as the other who challenges, as the enigmatic other, as the other who can signify diversion. More precisely, Paul Ricoeur speaks of an *errance,* a possibility of error, a motive for error. All this causes fear, an element of anguish. The important thing is to transform this relationship with this source of anguish, of challenge, of *errance,* to transform a potentially inimical relationship into a profoundly friendly one. And, I believe, that is a daily struggle.

Elsa: One last question, Julio. In many parts of Latin America you are best known for your book, *La Iglesia y el desafío de la pobreza* (Eng. trans.: *Good News to the Poor: The Challenge of the Poor in the History of the Church,* Orbis, 1979). If you had to write a book on the challenge of women to the church, particularly the Protestant churches, what would be its principal points?

Julio: I would start from my experience first of all with my wife and then with other women who have in one way or another been part of my life, that is, my wife as a profoundly intimate part of my being, my daughter, and other women, friends at work, poor women I have met. That's where I would start. And I would deal with themes, I would deal for example with the theme of God. The perception or the experience of God is not the same for women as for men. I have no doubt about this.

Nor is the experience of Jesus Christ or the Holy Spirit or the church. It's not a coincidence that the majority of churchgoers are women. I would raise an extremely important question. In the basic Christian communities of Brazil, with their millions of members, why are 80 or 85 percent of them women, poor women? I think it's because there is some freedom in these communities, which women do not find in the rest of society.

Then I would deal with the feminine in the Bible. I think of some women I met in Itaquera, struggling, hope-filled women, woman whom life had used. Often they were missing most of their teeth; they were sick. And it's those women who seem to me most like Mary, like Elizabeth. On the basis of this reality, which has its biblical expression, I would try to develop a theology.

But I would do this with fear and trembling, because I don't think that as I man I have the right to arrogate to myself the ability to speak of the feminine in theology. I think that women's challenge to the church must come principally from women. As a member of the sex that for so many centuries has dominated the life of the church, and that continues to dominate it, I think I need to be quiet. The principal challenge of women to the church is that the church should lose its fear of women, that men, who are in control, no longer should envy women because they were the first witnesses to the resurrection of Jesus Christ, and because they are the true protagonists of the people of God, since sociologically speaking, most of the people of God, the churchgoers, are women. But it is always men who are in charge of church administration.

When men are presented with the possibility of sharing with women in the life of the church, in an equal way, there are really pathological reactions. Saint Paul had a problem with women; there is no doubt of this. But the fact that Paul had a problem doesn't give us the right to continue to react to women the way he did. We need to react in a more normal way, without fear. I know it's one thing to say this and another to do it, but that's the challenge. When fear appears anguish also appears. And, as Kierkegaard says, anguish is the sign of sin, the sign that we are face-to-face with the world of death. Why should we be afraid and sense death in the presence of women? For isn't it with a woman that a man creates life?

I know that all this is a little unclear. I hadn't been asked this question before.

Elsa: I guess there's a good reason for it, don't you think? Thank you very much, Julio.

Jorge Pixley

San José, Costa Rica, December 1985

*It was interesting that Jorge did not want to be inter-
viewed alone. He brought his wife, Jenny, with him because, he said, she would help him be more sincere. But
even more interesting was that Jenny was worried that
Jorge would look like a male chauvinist in the interview,
so she reminded him that he always does the dishes. But
Jorge was most sincere, radically honest, just as he is in
his biblical analysis. The figure of Don Quixote on my
desk and the virgin of Da Vinci on the wall of my office
were my witnesses — as was Jenny. It was about 10 in the
morning.*

Elsa: Jorge, what has your experience been with your wife,
Jenny, and with your daughter? Do you consider yourself a
male chauvinist?

Jorge: As you know, my wife and daughter are the women who
are closest to me. And I have a granddaughter now, but she is
very young. I think our marriage is quite traditional in the way
we divide up the tasks. I don't cook unless Jenny is sick. I've
always helped with the cleaning, especially when the children
were young and there was more work to be done and we didn't
have any help at home, as we have since we've lived in Mexico.
So I don't think I've refused to do the homemaking chores, but
the division of our labor is more or less traditional.

20

[Jenny intervenes: "You always do the dishes."]

Jorge: It's true, I'm the one who always does the dishes. But what bothers me most is that marriage has provided a privileged position for me, especially in the choice of work, which has always been up to me and has involved our moving from one country to another several times. We've done this in accord with my capabilities, my interests, my understanding of my vocation. We've always discussed it, and Jenny has never opposed what we've done (in this sense I don't think I'm autocratic).

But it's always been in relationship to my sense of vocation and not hers. In her case I think her vocation has been more of a support for me, which is very traditional, and sometimes I... sometimes I feel... that it shouldn't be that way, but I don't know how to avoid it. I believe that our marriage has been mutually satisfying; it has helped us both. I don't think I've been dominating, consciously, that I've abused her or my daughter. But I realize that we participate in structures that give men privileges in our society, and we haven't been able to overcome this.

Elsa: And you're not in agreement with those structures.

Jorge: No, I'm not in agreement with those structures. I think they're unjust. But I think that the family is a very important social structure because it provides support, security. It's a space of support for the person, where there is a level of friendship, of fellowship, that we don't find outside the family. So I think it would be difficult simply to get rid of the family.

On the other hand I think that the family structure also necessarily imposes — and I don't know how to avoid it — the subjection of one person to another. And it doesn't have to be the woman to the man. In our case we have had the opportunity and felt the call to go from Puerto Rico to Mexico and from there to Nicaragua. These were dramatic steps requiring the reorientation of our life, and it would have been difficult for all the interests of both parties to be served.

And if there are children it's even more difficult. When we

moved from Puerto Rico to Mexico our daughter, Rebeca, who was sixteen at the time, had to leave all her friends behind and re-establish her life at an age when young people are quite insecure and don't make new friends easily or let new friends into their groups. We have to recognize that we did violence to Rebeca. That's one of the problems of the family.

Sometimes I've thought that to keep the family from becoming a straitjacket we need to find forms of divorce for cases where the lives of the two cannot be made compatible. And I've thought of this for us. It would be traumatic, of course, after twenty-seven years of marriage and three children, who are now grown, and a granddaughter and certainly other grandchildren to come. A separation of our lives would be traumatic, but it would be fairer to come to that than for one to impose on the other conditions that were unsatisfactory, unfulfilling. That is, if marriage is going to be an institution that satisfies and fulfills persons, divorce has to be a real possibility.

Elsa: Another possibility is to come to some understanding. It's been hard for me to come to such an agreement with my husband with regard to our doctoral studies. We have two children, and I can assure you that it's more difficult for the wife than for the husband.

Jorge: Of course.

Elsa: It took us four years to agree on the dates, the university, the country, and so forth. We both wanted to be happy and to be fulfilled, and we wanted our move to have the least possible negative effect on our children.

Jorge: I agree, that has to be the outcome.

Elsa: And if it's not, that's okay.

Jorge: Because the relationship between Jenny and me means a lot to me and to her as well. Divorce would be traumatic, really heart-breaking, but I think it has to be on our horizon. It has to be a real possibility so that one person is not tempted to force the other. At least that's how I see it.

Elsa: It also depends on Jenny's character. She could say, "I'm not going along with you this time. Why should I? I'm staying right here." Then I don't know what you'd do, right? A lot depends on the reaction of our spouse.

But let's move on to another question. Have you thought about how difficult it can be for a woman to read some of the antifeminist parts of the Bible? How would you approach the texts from a women's perspective? I think that not only women can read the Bible from a women's perspective, but men can as well.

Jorge: The first thing that comes to mind is the text in Ephesians that speaks of women. I think that it's irretrievable. I've never worked on it, but when I go to a wedding and I hear this passage, I find it very offensive. I would simply avoid it in a marriage ceremony. And if I had to interpret it I would have to say, as I have said in other instances and not only those pertaining to women, that such passages are not normative. It's like a discussion I had recently regarding Jeremiah and politics. I don't think that Jeremiah has to be a model for political activity or that I've failed as an interpreter if I don't find in him a politics that seems ideal, normative.

I'd have to say the same about Paul, or whoever was the author of Ephesians. My entire Christian experience leads me to reject his view of marriage. If that's what marriage is then we should abandon it. In one way or another human institutions should support persons and not destroy them. To say that women should subject themselves to their husbands is a way to deprive them of their dignity.

There are biblical texts that I think are simply unacceptable. So the interpretation has to revolve around recognition of this fact, and our vision of biblical authority has to include the possibility, the reality, that in the Bible there are some things that aren't Christian, to put it very crudely.

I'm quite sympathetic to the debate that's going on in the United States among feminists, that is, the tension that exists in the feminist movement between those who reject the Christian tradition and those who try to interpret it. It seems clear to me, and I think that some of the women would agree, that it is preferable to interpret the Bible in a way that exalts women, that enables them to develop, than it is to reject the Christian tradition. For the feminist movement to reject Christianity would mean to lose a great deal of cultural power, political power. But there's a lot in the Bible that makes rejection simpler, intellectually speaking.

As an interpreter of the Bible I share this dilemma; it's not a dilemma merely for women. In many biblical texts women are in a second-class position. I have written on the Exodus, which I consider a revolutionary, liberating movement. But one of the limitations of this movement is that it was unable to provide an appropriate role for women. The laws on adultery, although they are better than many others, even contemporary ones, are not just. A woman commits adultery if she has sexual relations outside marriage, but a man commits adultery only if his partner is married; this is not equal. Different criteria are used, although according to the law, with the limitation included in the definition of adultery, both are equally to blame.

Elsa: Jorge, could we set those texts aside if we chose to be guided by one of the central axes of the Bible, for example, that of oppression-liberation, God the Father, Jesus Christ, the Holy Spirit as accompanying the oppressed, as against oppression? In this way women, insofar as they are oppressed, or blacks, or indigenous people, could find liberating keys within the Bible itself when they identify themselves as oppressed subjects. The male chauvinist and racist passages could be considered peripheral, as part of the culture of that time.

Jorge: I agree with you on this. I think that the Bible presents certain instances that are germinal, that provide the basis for everything else in the Bible. I think that these are basically two: the Exodus and the life of Jesus Christ. Everything else has to be read in relation to these foundational narratives. I did say, though, that in the Exodus narrative there is a problem in regard to women, that is, justice is not done to women in the sense I have described. Exodus is the account of the liberation of a people. The same principle that is operative there and for which they are struggling in the political and economic sphere, in the laws of Sinai, can also be applied to the case of relationships between men and women. And it can be applied in a way that transcends the particular decrees of the law that exist in the Sinai code. I think that there is a norm, and it applies to many other spheres of life.

Any biblical text has to be read from the point of view of the God of the poor, the God of liberation. In many places it says that God is something else, for example, in Proverbs and in the book of Kings; there are many places that reflect a God who is not the God of the poor, the liberation God of the Exodus. But those passages have to be measured against the norm of the Exodus. In the New Testament the same could be said of certain passages in the Epistles that don't seem to reflect the preaching of the reign of God, of Jesus in the Synoptic Gospels. It seems to me that Jesus and his preaching of God's reign in the Synoptics has to be the norm that guides our reading and interpretation of everything else.

Elsa: Let's speak for a moment about the church. How do you view the participation of women in the Baptist church, or in the Protestant church as a whole?

Jorge: In the Baptist churches we have a traditional practice that puts women in second place in leadership functions in the church. There are few women who are pastors. There are some, but they are few. As far as I know, in Latin America only in Puerto Rico has there been a conscious effort to increase the number of women in the pastoral programs. In Mexico I didn't know of any. Women there are either missionaries or directors of Christian education. There are, of course, women's organizations in the churches and they have their projects, some of which are very important. For example, in the Baptist churches homes for the elderly are almost always women's responsibility. This is very important; if women didn't do it, we'd have to find some other way to do it.

Speaking of the Baptists in the United States, forty years ago women had their own missionary societies, both for home and foreign missions. These, I believe, were very important organizations, for they allowed women who were working as missionaries, whether with indigenous people or in inner-city work, to do so under the leadership of other women. All the executives and administrators of the society were women, as we have been able to learn from the histories written about the period. Often the women's missionary societies were more sensitive than the men's societies. Later, about 1948 or 1950, the two societies merged and I think that that was a loss, although there was a reason for it, a logic of efficiency. The merger meant that women were again second-class. In the United States today the function of the women's societies with regard to home and foreign mission work is financial support, the fund-raising base, and has ceased to play an active policy-making role as before. So we've moved backward during the past generation. I think the situation is similar in other churches.

Because of its symbolic value, I think that one of the keys is the role of women in ordained ministry. We have to promote it, and as a professor of theology this is one of the tasks I have to undertake.

Elsa: I think that at the same time we have to seek the renewal of the church, because even when the churches have women pastors they continue to be quite vertical in organization. We need a process of renewal. That is, the fundamental and primary struggle of women is not ordination, it seems to me, for that alone wouldn't bring about a change of the structure.

Jorge: I think it has a symbolic value.

Elsa: But not as the primary effort. I think it should be but one of the struggles.

Jorge: It's not a final goal, but I think it is an indispensable step for posing the problem in its true dimensions. That is, the prohibition of women's ordination is irrational.

Elsa: Yes.

Jorge: The ordained ministry has the symbolic value of leadership, of the one who speaks for the congregation. And if women are not allowed to do this I think we're legitimizing injustice within the church. Even if women are ordained as pastors, of course, this won't solve all the problems of inequality within the church. The vertical structure will continue to be a problem, but I think that the problem will be understood better.

As Baptists we have a democratic and anticlerical tradition, at least on a formal level. I think we have to take advantage of this and change it from a formal democracy into a real community where all of us participate in the decisions of the church, in the church's celebrative life, and in all other church activity. So I think we have a tradition that can be recuperated. Even more, the formal structures are less oppressive than in other churches where women's ordination is not permitted and they cannot administer the sacraments.

Elsa: Thank you very much, Jorge.

Hugo Assmann

San José, Costa Rica, December 1985

Hugo came to San José for a meeting of economists and theologians, and I took advantage of the opportunity to interview him. We talked in my office at the Seminario Bíblico Latinoamericano. Hugo was very serious. He is usually quite the joker, but not this time. Before the interview he showed me a newspaper clipping on women and asked if it was okay to mention it. I said that if he wanted to it was okay, but he forgot. During the interview I realized the depth of Hugo's analysis of the women's issue. Witness to our conversation was a papier-mâché Don Quixote on my desk, holding up a book with one hand and grasping a sword with the other. It was about 8:30 in the morning.

Elsa: Hugo, I'm going to ask a question that might seem to be very simple, but it can lead to some interesting discussion: Do you think that women are oppressed in Latin America?

Hugo: Women's oppression has different characteristics. First, there is the overall oppression of women as women, independently of their social class. I don't think we can reduce the oppression of women to the oppression of poor women, of women of the poor classes. There is a general oppression of women, and it is very widespread and effective even in the middle and upper classes. But this isn't the point that I want to stress,

28

although I do think that when we analyze women's oppression among the poorer classes we also have to look to the patriarchal roots of our society; and these do not depend uniquely and exclusively on the configuration of our society, that is, on the model of capitalist production. The roots of the oppression go further back, although under capitalism oppression takes on very specific characteristics.

Second, over and above this general oppression of women there is a whole series of new and very tragic dimensions to the oppression of women in the lower classes. In other words, women of the oppressed classes are not only doubly but triply oppressed, or even worse. Lower-class women suffer not only the oppression that all dominated people suffer in a class society; as women the greatest burden of that overall class oppression falls on them. We need to broaden our analysis. What does this double oppression of women mean, women oppressed as women, and women oppressed as members of the dominated class? I don't think that women should see themselves simply as members of the oppressed class. For by the very fact of being women in that class they suffer a double oppression.

But there is a third dimension to the oppression of women, namely, oppressed men are still oppressive men. I don't think we can simply dilute this third dimension into a simple class analysis, as has often been done, where this special dimension of women's oppression disappears. As members of the oppressed class poor women already carry a great burden of oppression. But in addition in the oppressed classes there is also reproduced man-woman oppression, often in very specific forms. Women are oppressed by their men, their partners, and by male society in general, at the heart of the oppressed classes.

Let me give an example. I was recently on the committee of a doctoral dissertation at a university in Brazil. The subject was *boiafria* women. These are seasonal workers who find occasional work harvesting coffee, cutting sugar cane, etc. *Boiafria* women are different from *boiafria* men in many ways. First, women are paid less than men for the same work. Second, many think that the women cannot produce as much and so they suffer in labor relations. The brokers are much crueler toward the women in levying production quotas.

This is an indication of how women are not only oppressed as women in the lower classes. They carry a greater burden, not only at home, where they have a double schedule since they have to do the household chores that men will often not do. In the workplace itself they are discriminated against because they are not given equal pay for equal work, even though they often do the work better. I'm thinking of the service sector and salaried workers. Men who clean buildings like schools earn much more than women who do the same job. This is what I meant when I said that women as members of the oppressed class are doubly discriminated against as women.

But there is another point, and here I want to refer to the dissertation on the language of the *boiafria* women. The destruction of women's bodiliness, the destruction of their freedoms and gestures, their freedom of movement, their freedom of options with regard to friendship and love, their language for speaking about themselves, their possessions, their work world, their family world, all this is a complex reality invaded by what could be called a castration of languages. When we speak of the castration of languages we must understand that we are not referring solely to the capacity to reflect and express thought. We are rather referring to corporal language, gestural language, the ability to express oneself; and we are also referring to verbal language. That is, women's vocabulary is in part destroyed, but even more thoroughly destroyed is the gestural world, that of non-inhibition.

Let me provide a concrete example. In the oppressed classes there is a repression of women's spontaneity in expressing their feelings in the marriage relationship. Men want to control the rhythm of pleasure, and women are oppressed even with regard to the most intimate aspects of spontaneity. This has very serious implications, because women almost necessarily have to resort to forms of self-defense, of resistance, that are often unconscious. To survive women even begin to collaborate in the game of their own destruction. They begin to accept the patterns of domination applied to their erotic life. They no longer exercise their right to a free expression of their erotic pleasure.

In the dissertation I mentioned, which was based on extensive field work, the data are frankly astonishing. Women are reduced to accommodation, to mini-hopes, because even the hope to develop oneself as a person in moments of intense joy are nullified. In other words, their erotic space, their erotic time-duration, is sharply reduced, reduced to a few years, reduced to very few occasions. And we cannot understand the more social and political dimensions of oppression if we don't also analyze these very profound forms it takes.

I want to touch on one other point. What happens — and here we have a very tragic situation — when women begin to participate in movements that have as one of their goals the liberation of women? And we needn't be thinking of sophisticated organizations. What happens then? In many cases we can suppose a certain initial inhibition to speak about themselves. But later these women, who often are very active in the popular movements, in the basic communities, begin to move, and they move at a much quicker pace than the men, than their partners.

What happens when the men are left behind? I think it's very difficult to analyze this, but it's possible that the men are now provided with new motives for new oppression of women. They begin to pull in the reins, they begin to think that it's not such a good idea that the women should be mixed up in this kind of thing. They are envious. But there's also an underlying guilt, a kind of fear perhaps of consequences unconsciously foreseen. How am I going to be challenged if she continues like this? What am I going to have to change in my life? This doesn't happen on a very rational level, but it is very real.

So then women begin to meet as women, to discuss women's problems with other women. The men are involved with other things and are not part of the discussion. There is even a social division over priorities in some very excellent projects, grass-

roots work, political work, etc. All of a sudden the men have
other priorities, while the women begin to discover the importance of their specific oppression. And it's very difficult for the
men to understand.

But not only is it difficult for men to understand; it is also
insufficient, for rational awareness is not enough. Suppose that
a man, of any social class, middle class, oppressed class, has it
all very clear in his head, a mental clarity about the oppression
of women, and about his role as a man brought up to be part
of that oppression. From this realization to an effective transformation of behavior there is quite a distance. You don't get
rid of machismo by becoming aware of it.

I think there might be something wrong when women begin
to discuss their problems by themselves. It's even worse when
they undertake plans for their liberation along their own paths,
leaving the men out. I'm not very clear about this, but I don't
think that it's always harmful for women to want to pursue their
own liberation somewhat apart from men, because things move
too slowly if men are always around. Women have to create
their associative power to become stronger. But I think there
really has to be dialogue, because if there is none, the men's
world does not change and this can mean that the strategy for
the liberation of women can be truncated.

Elsa: Hugo, what would happen to the church if women par-
ticipated in a significant way? Would it be a different church?
And another question having to do with theology: If there were
as many women as men doing theology in Latin America, would
theological discourse be the same or would there be changes?

Hugo: I'd like to try to look at this question dispassionately,
forgetting the fact that finally there are some women's voices
speaking out more openly in the Latin American church and in
Latin American theology. This is quite significant, although it is
just beginning; the numbers are still very small. Your question
goes much deeper. Would the church be different if women's
participation were greater? First, Elsa, I think we need to be

clear about one thing, and that's what I meant when I spoke of dispassionate analysis. Women's participation is already very great in terms of work load, for example, in my church, the Catholic church, if by participation — and here's where words can fool us — we mean who does what. Compare the numbers of men and women involved in church work.

Elsa: No, I was referring to decision making...

Hugo: Yes, I know. There are many more women than men in the church, and there's the tragedy. There are more women, they do more work, they carry the greater burden, for example, in the area of religious instruction. In catechesis, in evangelization, the number of women involved is huge; it is much greater than the number of men. But this raises the other issue all the more, namely, the fact that there is no recognition of women's ministries. I'm not speaking here of priesthood. I don't think there's any biblical reason why women should not be ordained and at some point women will have to insist on it, but I'm not sure it's a priority. The problem is that women are given no ministerial rights on any level. There's not even a theology of the priesthood of all believers spelled out in terms of women's ministries in the church. They are always subjected to male ministerial bosses. But as the actual doers of the work there are more women. In our church, the number of active women, struggling women, is incredibly large. Their generosity is very impressive.

So we have to ask, when will it all explode? If women are in the majority and the explosion doesn't occur — I'm trying to look at this dispassionately — that gives us an idea of the many levels that need to be analyzed to deal with this concentration of male minority power. Their power seems so great that it can't be destroyed. And if it's not, women will never participate on ministerial levels, and I'm not referring just to ordination but to decision making. No matter how much we work for liberation the church won't change.

Under the present power arrangements in the church, the

sacrament of orders is monopolized and controlled by men, with all the consequences of this. I think it's very important that this power can to a certain extent be turned to the benefit of the poor. There are certain figures in the church in Latin America who have demonstrated this, and we consider them to be prophets and martyrs, like Bishop Oscar Romero and some others, although their number is small. But there is a much more serious problem, the absence of women on the decision-making levels of the church, and this occurs even when the church is the servant of the poor. This oppression must be eliminated. I don't think this is a problem of only secondary importance, and we are still far from getting at the heart of it.

With regard to theology I'm glad to see that you yourself and some other women are following a theological vocation, but frankly I think we're only at the beginning. We have to quicken the pace, but I'm not very clear about how to go about this, and I'm not so sure that it's up to the male theologians to do this.

Elsa: I was wondering if you think that theological discourse would change if there were many women doing theology.

Hugo: Very well, I want to speak about theological discourse, but allow me to finish what I was saying. I think that we have a problem here, and perhaps the men who are conscious of it should use all the power we have within the male structures of the church to open more doors to women theologians. Because realistically it is not always possible for them to do it alone. In the training of women theologians and exegetes I have a serious concern. Nearly all the centers where women can go for training are controlled by men. So women need to be very clear about their vocation; it is not only their vocation as theologians in general, but also their vocation as women theologians.

Would the language of theology change? I think that not only would language change, but semantic priority as well. Certain themes would have priority and others that are now considered very important would become less important.

Elsa: I think that the way of doing theology would change as well.

Hugo: The way meaning the subject of theology? the way of communication? the way of language? What are you referring to when you speak of ways?

Elsa: Some Latin American women have come to realize that the logical, rational method is not the only one for doing theology; there are other ways.

Hugo: What you say is very important, and I think that here there is a contribution that only women can make. But we need to be careful, for male theologians might then say, "Very well, there are different ways of doing theology. There are more rational languages and there are more poetic languages. We'll leave the more poetic languages to the women, and we'll use the more rational." We must not fall into that trap. All of us, men and women, have to realize that there are different languages, various forms of understanding and communication. That's why I'm so glad to see, and I want to mention this explicitly here, that Rubem Alves is working with a poetico-ludic theology, with a language itself freighted with utopia. This task belongs not only to women. I think that women's contribution is very important, but if women say, "This is our contribution," we'll fall into a trap, because I believe that women can have a rational intelligence just as men can.

Elsa: Of course.

Hugo: I think this is a general problem that affects both men and women theologians.

Elsa: It has to do with our westernized culture...

Hugo: ...where we believe that the only way to know is the logical, rational way, but I don't even think that this is the most perfect form of understanding. In terms of human experience, I have to confess, I've learned a lot from books, but I really think I've learned much more in the university of life. These are forms of understanding that penetrate very deeply into our minds, but much more into the totality of our entire being. This is a very, very important subject.

Elsa: Hugo, in some of your writing you mention women's issues. Speaking concretely, how do you integrate women into your life?

Hugo: I'll tell you, Elsa, that it's much easier said than done. This is another case where to have things clearly in our minds doesn't mean we know how to live them. For me *compañeras* that I'm close to signify grace embodied in the circumstances of history. It is a challenging and costly grace that enables us to move ahead; without this kind of relationship we move ahead only along rational paths. We move a little, but not enough.

I feel a little inhibited to say any more about this because I would have to speak on a personal level. I have a partner who has helped me very much, and, frankly, if there's any balance in my life I owe it in large measure to her. There are many things that never would have occurred to me if it hadn't been for suggestions she's given me in conversations and even in moments of meditation, of joy together.

I must confess that there are things that seem impossible for me to accomplish in what remains of my career as sociologist and theologian. The next generation will have to advance far beyond us, not only on the level of exposition and reflection on the topic, but on the level of experience in general. I hope that in the future there will be couples in which both partners are theologians, in which men and women exegetes share their lives together, associated in a kind of quest to write, to produce texts. And the texts will come out differently.

Formalism and ritualization in prayer and spirituality is compatible with a kind of male-female division of roles. And based on my experience it is my deep conviction that the time has come in history that we have to say quite forcefully that a spirituality for men and a spirituality for women, each separate, must be transcended. I think that true spirituality must be profoundly penetrated by the shared life of men and women. This would be a spirituality along the lines of the Song of Songs. I think we've come to the end of the chapter on "my spirituality as a man" and "my spirituality as a woman." We have to have an interchange. There is great enrichment in this, which I have been able to take advantage of only a little through the years of living with my partner.

Elsa: You're right, Hugo. But I still think that we are in a process of a liberating re-reading of that first chapter, so that the next step that you mention can really be one of mutual enrichment. Women want to be different and even note the difference. I get the impression that to speak at this time of equality is to speak of masculinity. We don't want to be men; at least I don't.

Hugo: I was going to come to that. I think that the equality thesis is a liberal bourgeois thesis. Just as in the social order, in the political order it is a preambular thesis, that is, a thesis referring to minimum basic aspirations. We speak of equality of rights and things like that, but this is not a profound anthropological perspective, much less a Christian one. In a Christian perspective we must go beyond equality to speak of otherness and specificity. If that is nullified I think there is no longer even any complementary enrichment.

Elsa: ... but rather everything is masculine.

Hugo: Right.

Elsa: Since it's men who are in control. To finish, Hugo, say something about the Bible.

Hugo: In thirty or forty years, I think, we'll see the Bible differently because of the contributions of women. For example, look at the origins of Christianity. When will we begin to admit that in Jesus' movement the presence of women was absolutely decisive? We could even say that at the beginning in Galilee, for example, it was the women who sustained the continuity of the movement. How is it that in early Christianity, with such a feminine presence, masculine patterns were very quickly established?

This re-reading of the origins of Christianity seems very important to me, like every re-reading of the history of the church from a different point of view, not only from the viewpoint of the oppressed, but also from the viewpoint of oppressed women. And this re-reading will enable us to discover wonderful things. The re-reading of the Bible in this perspective is still a great gap.

I want to conclude by saying that I think there's a whole history of spirituality, of women's contributions to spirituality, that still remains to be written. Every once in a while there is some outstanding, unforgettable figure, but there is a history of prophetic, spiritual contributions of women down through history that still has not been written.

Elsa: It's true, we have to construct it and reconstruct it. Thank you very much, Hugo.

Gustavo Gutiérrez

Lima, Peru, January 1986

*On a Sunday in January I went with my tape recorder to
the Mass that Gustavo Gutiérrez was celebrating with a
basic Christian community. It was good to see him in his
priestly vestments with bread and wine in his hands. He
winked at me from the altar, and then at the kiss of peace
we greeted each other with an abrazo and agreed on a time
to meet. After Mass I went with him to the hospital to
visit a bishop who was sick. Then Carmen Lora took us
home, and there in a little office full of books and papers
we cleared a space to speak about women. As he spoke
I thought that Gustavo is truly our "guru," as we have
called him since our visit to India. The interview ended
when Carmen called us to lunch. It was about 2 o'clock
in the afternoon.*

Elsa: Gustavo, from reading your books and just from seeing
the way you are, I know that you are very sensitive to people's
suffering, to their oppression. And I think that this extends
to women's oppression as well. But still I want to ask you, is
the oppression of women a reality? Tell me something about
yourself and your experience with women.

Gustavo: Unfortunately the reality of women's oppression is
obvious. And what is most serious is that many of the causes
for the oppression are rooted deeply in human beings, in men

39

but in women as well, on a subconscious level. There are ways of living, ways of understanding things, that at root consider women to be inferior. I don't think I'm saying anything new here; this is what many women have been saying and with good reason. For example, it seems to me that in most families, especially in relatively poor families, the education of the sons is more important than the education of the daughters. I experienced this in my own family. I was much more important in my family because I was a safer investment for the support of the family and perhaps for the progress that every family aspires to, material progress, that is. There were three children and I was the only son. I went to school when I was very young, I liked it, I studied, that is, I was more or less responding to my parents' concern. My sisters went to school as well, but there was much more concern for me than for them. And this attitude is so deeply rooted that it seemed normal; everybody accepted it. It was my parents' attitude, but my sisters accepted it. I think there is something very profound involved here.

When we speak of the oppression of women, I think we have to speak especially — not exclusively but especially — of the oppression of poor women. This has been our perspective in the theology of liberation. There is an expression that is very well known today, "doubly oppressed and marginalized," which we managed to get included in the Puebla document.* And I believe that in fact women are doubly marginalized and doubly oppressed, both because they are poor and because they are women. It is not only a matter of oppression, of disdain for the person herself, for women are considered inferior by the very fact of being women. But there are two other issues involved.

First, like any profound oppression, the oppression of women damages all of society in an intolerable way. Not only are women marginalized and oppressed, but also a sick human society re-

---

*Unfortunately, this expression was put in a footnote to the final edited document of the 1979 bishops' conference at Puebla, Mexico, although it had been in the main body of the approved text. But at least it is there, in paragraph 1134.

sults. There are repercussions. I know that this is also true for other kinds of oppression, social oppression, oppression in employment, etc., precisely because these too are profound. But I want to emphasize — and again this is not new — that the oppression of women is not peripheral to society, it is not a peripheral oppression, but is at the very center of its meaning.

Second, not only must we be sensitive to the intolerable situation of women in society today, but we must also be sensitive to all that human society is losing because of this oppression. I'm very afraid that by speaking of their oppression we will approach women in a condescending way: "The poor little thing is so marginalized and oppressed, we need to help her out." I think that we need to join in solidarity with women's demands because otherwise we miss out on too much ourselves. I know that this is a nuance to what I am saying, but I have experienced this in a very deep way.

I want to add one more thing. The first sentence in *A Theology of Liberation* (pardon me for quoting myself) reads, "This book . . . is based on the Gospel and the experiences of men and women . . . of Latin America." When I gave the manuscript to some friends to read, they laughed at me because they didn't see why I had to say "women." They considered the experience of men to be the experience of the human race. But I thought it was very important to specify that it came out of the experiences of men and women, the experience of oppression, but also the experience of struggle, of the values that men and women bear within that oppression.

Elsa: Gustavo, my second question has to do with women and the church. I know that this is a little difficult for you, as a Catholic priest and theologian, under present ecclesial circumstances. Do you think that the present structure of the church is unjust toward women and should be changed? Tell us how you see the presence and participation of women in the basic Christian communities.

Gustavo: There are lights and shadows here. I think that the

church is partly responsible for the profound disdain that we see
for women, this non-consideration of feminine values. Whether
this was done with the best of intentions or not, we need not
discuss here. Some might not like to admit this, but it is a
fact. I think that the church has contributed to the problem,
justifying its position with a series of arguments, including the
Bible. For in the Bible itself there are a number of expressions
and concepts that have supported such a position throughout
the history of the Christian community. And this is true in the
various Christian denominations as well.

On the other hand, it is also true that Christianity has contributed to an appreciation of women. That is why I said there
have been some lights. But to dwell on what the church has contributed to an understanding and appreciation of women seems
ingenuous to me, because the church has also contributed to a
devaluing of women. And I think that even today in the church
women do not formally play the role that is theirs as equal human beings.

When we consider the basic ecclesial communities, we find
some little surprises, because in the daily work of these communities women play a very important role, often much more
important than that of the men.

I'm not speaking only about women as being more interested
in religion, as some would say. I'm referring to their tenac-
ity, their creativity, their closeness to the suffering of humanity.
And this they have in abundance, because — whether by society's virtue or society's defect — they are placed in situations
that allow them to be very close to human suffering. For this
reason women will fight for certain things much harder than
men. And in the basic Christian community, the role of women
is very important. So that when I say that in the church, in
the institution, in a formal sense women do not have the responsibility that they should, it is correct. But it is also true
that in a number of ways they have purely and simply taken
responsibility.

I really cannot conceive of the popular Christian communities without women, and I am not speaking theoretically. You can see it in any meeting. In the parish where I work, for example, women have a central role in a whole range of parish activities. This is not enough, I know. Women are still not allowed to fulfill certain roles in the church. But at the same time they in fact play a very important role. There are many reasons for this, but I believe the fundamental one is women's closeness to suffering and their capacity for struggle. I think that men have received from society certain categories, certain ways to behave, that make them evade reality. But women, and I am speaking here of women of the popular classes, poor women are very much closer to many things. Perhaps this explains women's central role in the basic ecclesial communities.

Elsa: You mention women's closeness to suffering. Consuelo del Prado, a theologian working in Peru, points this out in her article "Yo siento a Dios de otro modo" ("I experience God in a different way"). This brings us to the question of spirituality. You have written a book entitled *Beber en su propio pozo* (*We Drink from Our Own Wells,* Orbis, 1984), in which you introduce us to spirituality. I think you would agree with this expression of Arguedas, "I experience God in a different way," when a poor person speaks vis-à-vis a rich person. But can a woman say the same thing, as a woman? In other words, can we speak of spirituality from a women's perspective?

Gustavo: I think so. In fact when Arguedas uses the expression he is referring to a woman. In his novel *Todas las sangres,* it is a woman who says, "I experience God in a different way." I have worked through that expression and dealt with it in a short study I did of Arguedas.

Here there is a very important question of sensitivity. In Arguedas, the woman is to a certain extent the human being with the virtues that he prefers: strength, dignity, tenderness. There are several very interesting passages in Arguedas. I think that Consuelo's use of this expression to speak of spirituality is very rich indeed. It enables us to see, in fact, that there is a spirituality already being born in Latin America. This is my thesis in *We Drink from Our Own Wells:* There is a spiritual experience being born in Latin America. Within that spirituality there are many nuances and inflections, as we might expect, that correspond to the differences to be found among the poor. That is, we can speak of the poor, but as soon as we have spoken of the poor we have to say that they are of one color or another, that they are men or women; among the poor there a variety of aspects, inflections, special nuances. I think that this is also the case with regard to spiritual experience. That is what Consuelo is saying: how, as a woman, can one live a relationship with God and with others, or, in other words, how, as a woman. can one find a way to be Christian. And this is a spirituality.

We are not saying that women have a way of being Christian totally different from men; we are all human beings. This relates to what I was saying a moment ago, that we should not be concerned in a condescending way but rather so that we not continue to be deprived of these universal human values. For various reasons women can be the bearers of these values, but they are values for everyone. We are speaking of a nuance in spirituality that women can contribute and reveal to us. The gift is revealed in the first place to other women, because women are deeply affected by a macho ideology and so are not aware of this dimension of their spirituality. And this gift is revealed to men as well. But women reveal this not only as a "feminine" characteristic, but rather as a human characteristic, and so it challenges men too.

We are speaking of a way for men to be Christian too. I want to insist on this point because otherwise we can begin to think that the spirituality born among the poor can be divided into numerous spiritualities: black spirituality, mestizo spirituality, Indian spirituality, women's spirituality. I think this is naïve. I don't want to impose a unity here but I think that there is a complex unity involved. There is a profound spirituality of the poor centered on the death/life dialectic. Faced with their own death/life dialectic, even in the biological sense, women experience something that men do not. And they remind all of us of its meaning; their contribution is for everyone.

I think therefore that to enter deeply into the spiritual journey of women is to enter deeply into the spiritual journey of human beings; theirs is a contribution. There is a profound richness here and we are just at its very beginnings. In my book *We Drink from Our Own Wells* sometimes I say that a spirituality "is being born" and other times I say, "I don't know if it is being born." It is in a very embryonic state. I think the same about this deepening of the special journey of women. We can go much further.

Elsa: Gustavo, for some time feminists reacted against and rejected certain values like tenderness and self-denial that society assigned to women par excellence. We considered them to be stereotypes. They were commonly held to be inferior to values like rationality, calmness, objectivity. But I have noticed that recently Latin American women, in the search for their identity, want to appropriate or reassert tenderness, play, affection, as profoundly rich traits of women, and to link these with strength, courage, bravery, which are also, in fact, rich traits of women. I think that these values should be reappropriated, reinterpreted without prejudice, and because they are to be found in such abundance in women, although not exclusively in them, they might be some of the contributions we can make along the path of our liberation. We can help men achieve a greater degree of sensitivity in the concrete situations of life. What do you think about this?

Gustavo: I want to say something about that. I can understand this reaction against the values assigned by society to women as part of a kind of poetic, agreeable contempt. One day a woman is a goddess and the next day she's a servant. But values like tenderness, I want to repeat, are values of humankind as a whole. As a man I personally do not want to renounce tenderness. I don't consider it women's private possession. And I think it quite serious when men with such a mentality want nothing to do with such things, because they think of them as women's matters, as inferior.

I think that if women are appreciated and give a certain savor to tenderness, this can liberate many men from their refusal to recognize that they also experience tenderness and should experience it. That's what I mean when I say that these contributions liberate us. And that is what I meant before about a sick society. When we deny ourselves such a gift we become sick. And I think that men's lives are deformed if they think that tenderness is alien to men. But this is what we find in a macho mentality that deforms both men and women. It is a mentality that not only disdains women; it also deforms men as human beings.

Elsa: A final question on the methodology of the theology of liberation. I have said elsewhere that for me the methodology of liberation theology allows us to do theology from a women's perspective. And this is not only because it considers women an object of reflection, but also because it gives them space to be the active subjects of the theological task. That is, the theology of liberation will have to appropriate the oppression of women, as it has the oppression of blacks and indigenous peoples, to be faithful to its methodology. It takes the reality of oppression as its starting point and it seeks a transformation of that reality. What do you think?

Gustavo: I think that is correct. I am increasingly convinced that in the theology of liberation the question of the theological task, of how we do theology, is a central point.

In the case of a theology from a women's perspective, to take a certain reality as a starting point and to reflect upon it and from within it is a central tenet of our methodology. That is what a feminist theology can and ought to do. It is therefore certainly not strange that feminist theology today, not only in Latin America but throughout the world, is situated within the framework of the theology of liberation. Sometimes we might disagree over one or another point, especially when the theology originates in the richer societies. But generally theology from a feminist perspective is part of the overall framework of the theology of liberation.

Previously feminist theology could not find an appropriate framework, purely and simply because to be a woman is a way to be poor. We never have a very clear and complete definition of "poor," but for me to be poor means to be insignificant, to have no importance, or rather to have no importance that is recognized by the dominant classes, by the powerful. Such is the case for the poor, for the indigenous peoples, for women. Women are the insignificant ones of history. And so we speak of a double oppression that in this case means double insignificance.

But I would also link this point about theological methodology to something we were saying about spirituality, for as time goes by I am increasingly convinced that our methodology is our spirituality. Our starting point is the first act, that of commitment to the poor. And as a second act we reflect on this commitment. This is not only a technical question, but it is also a way to be Christian. For me this is a spirituality. Christians are those who are committed to the poor and reflect on that commitment. It is a way of being, and therefore what we were saying about spirituality holds true here as well. I think that not only is there a link between methodology and spirituality. I'm beginning to see that there is a certain identification of the two. This is one of the central ideas of my little book on Job.*

Elsa: And in *We Drink from Our Own Wells.*

Gustavo: Yes. The first act is to be a Christian, to believe in the Lord, to be committed to others. This is to be a Christian and this is spirituality. What else is spirituality but this? In chapter 2 of *We Drink from Our Own Wells* I deal more with the question of the path; we have to reflect on the following of Jesus. My path for doing theology is inscribed in my path for

---

* *Hablar de Dios desde el sufrimiento del inocente;* Eng. trans.: *On Job: God-Talk and the Suffering of the Innocent* (Orbis, 1987).

being a Christian. I consider this at length in Job. For all practical purposes the book of Job is centered on this theme of the identification, I would say, between methodology and spirituality.

Job raises the question of theological method. And so the title of the book is *Hablar de Dios,* "To speak of God," "God-talk." Because the big problem in the book of Job is how we can speak of God from the standpoint of those who suffer in innocence, like Job. And this is our question in Latin America. To speak of God is to do theology.

Elsa: And the new experience of God is very clear. Job comes to see new faces of God that he had not seen before.

Gustavo: That's right, that's right. I think that the themes of suffering, gratuitousness, justice, and so forth are central in Job, but they revolve around this theme of spirituality and methodology. That's why I think it is such an important reflection. Until Paul, Job is the person in the Bible who most insists on the gratuitousness of the love of God. It is Job who carries this the furthest, starting from the human case in which it is most difficult to understand the gratuitousness of God, namely, suffering. Parodoxically, suffering is the most difficult case for understanding gratuitousness. For in the face of suffering either we resign ourselves, which is not to recognize gratuitousness, or we become cynical or depressed or self-centered. Those who suffer sometimes fall into the temptation of feeling like the center of the world and everyone has to ask how they are and how their troubles are going. Job takes the most difficult human case, I think, and there speaks of the gratuitousness of the love of God. So I think that the question of methodology is very closely linked to spirituality.

Elsa: Thank you very much, Gustavo.

José Míguez Bonino

Chaclacayo, Peru, January 1986

I had to attend a meeting on evangelization sponsored by the Methodist church in Lima. On my way I stopped in Panama and bought a small tape recorder because I knew that José Míguez Bonino would be at the meeting as well. On the fifth day we were able to get away and went to a place where there were some swings. We sat on a large swing that had room enough for both of us. Míguez was very peaceful and content, like the afternoon and myself. Unfortunately I was not able to record the sunshine, the color of the flowers, or the smiles of the people. The most I could capture was the squeaking of the chains on the swing — which I didn't transcribe. It was about 4:30 in the afternoon.

Elsa: Míguez, do you think that women's oppression is real? Tell to me a little about your personal experience as a married Protestant theologian.

Míguez: Of course women's oppression is real, and it appears in different ways on every level of society. The first thing I thought of when you asked about oppression was what happened to a young woman who used to come once a week to take care of our house while we were away. My wife and I returned home from vacation to find her with her eye swollen, her arms and chest bruised, her face cut. Her husband had found her in the

49

street and had given her a beating. This phenomenon of physical punishment of women is very common in our society and not only among the poorer classes. It has different expressions on different levels of society.

But to experience oppression requires a certain level of consciousness. In my neighborhood in Puerto de Rosario, where I grew up, women said that their husbands had the right to hit them because they were men, that is, they didn't experience the beating as oppression. This young woman who worked in our home, however, did indeed experience it as oppression, because she had developed a certain consciousness of her rights, of the respect due her.

So we must distinguish between the oppression of women, which is universal in our culture and others as well, and of the experience of that oppression, which becomes subjective only when there is a certain level of awareness. And we need to ask whether our Christian faith as it is lived in our communities helps in the development of this awareness or not.

As for my experience as a married theologian, I wonder how much we are agents of the oppression of women in a predetermined way, independently of whether we want to be or not, predetermined by the way things work. My wife, for example, has great artistic talent, a very fertile imagination. She could have been an actress, but she couldn't develop this talent when she was a child nor as an adolescent. This was partly due to the religious atmosphere, or rather religious prejudice, in her home, where artist and sinner were practically synonymous terms. And she wasn't able to develop it later simply because her situation as the wife of a pastor, theologian, or professor didn't allow for it. To what degree was my work itself oppressive for her, since when our children were young I often had to travel as part of my work at the school of theology? She repressed her own creativity.

I never thought about it at the time, and, even more interesting, she didn't either. We both considered it perfectly natural. But now we have become aware of this.

Elsa: What does she say now when you say that you both have become aware of it?

Míguez: She now realizes what she could have done but didn't. And I wouldn't say that she resents it, but she does feel it. I think we are just now realizing how much the limitations on women are part and parcel of the way society works. It's not simply a question of a change in attitude. Attitude change is necessary, but I think it is important to confront the mechanisms in our society that cause discrimination and oppression of women to occur almost automatically.

Elsa: Let's move on to talk about women and the church. Míguez, what has been the Methodist church's attitude toward women? How do women participate in the church? Is their presence significant or are there problems here?

Míguez: Numerically women have always been an important part of the church, and in most of the churches women are in the majority. Women have been active, but it seems clear to me that they have also been excluded even in the Methodist church, which is liberal in its operation, or at least there has never been proscription of women even on a ministerial level. We have had women fully participating in ministry for many years.

But it is interesting that women have almost had to create for themselves within our church their own church where they could be the protagonists. I refer to the women's societies. For a long time there were protests because the women's societies were separate: they had their own finances, their own worship services, their own publications, their own programs, their own federation on local, regional, national, and continental levels, their own ecumenical movement. We didn't ask why such a "parallel church" had been created, but I think it was created because in the church as a whole women were being assigned the subordinate roles: women organized the teas, the parties, occasionally they were Sunday school teachers. But in church administration they had subordinate roles. So women created, they had to create, a place where they could really be subjects.

The Methodist women's societies were for a long time called "auxiliaries." They were accepted, but only as auxiliary, second-class organizations. On the other hand it was in the women's societies that women developed their leadership abilities, which later broke into the life of the church. In the Methodist church today, at least in Argentina, in all the organizations in the church, women are numerically fairly represented, sometimes more than half, sometimes less. And this is without any quotas or regulations requiring it. With regard to the ordained ministry, experience has shown that there is no discrimination. They are accepted like any other pastor.

Elsa: I know that Nelly Ritchie, a pastor and theologian, is the superintendent of a large region.

Míguez: Yes, right now three of our eight superintendents are women. It's interesting that the nominations of the four or five women who were proposed came from every part of the country, that is, in every part of the country these persons were considered as worthy candidates for superintendent. Also interesting is the unity that the candidates felt among themselves. They met and together decided who would accept and who would decline the positions. They believed that they were women ministers within the overall ministry of the church and that they had to formulate their own strategy to assure that their work would have the greatest impact.

Elsa: This phenomenon that we find in the church of Argentina is not so apparent in other Methodist churches in Latin America, for example in Mexico or Central America.

Míguez: Yes, I think that's true.

Elsa: There doesn't seem to be any consistency among the Protestant churches.

Míguez: I don't know that much about the other churches. But I do want to add an interesting point about our church in Argentina. I think that women also play an important role in the development of ecumenical initiatives. As I mentioned they have had their own ecumenical movement. Even before other church groups did so, women and young people developed their own ecumenical organizations with their own publications and programs. And there developed a community, a relationship among women of different churches who got to know each other, visiting back and forth, that their congregations as such did not experience. This has been going on with women's and youth groups since the thirties, and it has had an important impact in the federation of churches. In recent years in Argentina under the military, Christian groups have been quite militant in defense of human rights, both in specifically church movements and in the broader human rights movement, like, for example, the Permanent Assembly, or the organizations of family members of detained and missing persons; women have had an outstanding role in these movements. And then, of course, there are the mothers of the Plaza de Mayo.*

Elsa: Míguez, you have written many books, and among other things, you are one of the Protestant theologians who has dealt with justification by faith. My question is this: How would you recast this subject from a women's perspective?

Míguez: One of our problems is that we still don't know what a "women's perspective" is. What's the difference between the way men and women address different subjects? Are the differences due to real differences between men and women? Or are they due to the roles that they have played in society, which have created different ways of thinking, of conceiving things, of relating to the world, of qualitatively and quantitatively evaluating things. That is, the modality or the viewpoint of the feminine perspective will be apparent only to the degree that women have full access to the totality of human activity and so are able to recreate this feminine modality. I am very curious to know, for example, what is going to happen to the concep-

---

*Mothers of missing persons, presumed detained or dead, who regularly staged protests in the Plaza de Mayo in Buenos Aires.

tion and exercise of pastoral ministry when half the pastors, or even a third, have been women over a period of twenty years. What formulation, what reconception of the ministry, will be produced by the presence of women over a period during which they can fashion their own way of doing things? This will be extremely significant.

To get back to your question, let me answer in a somewhat tentative, imaginative way. For in the first place I'm not a woman, and in the second I'm not sure how much we can talk about a women's perspective. But I do think that one of the characteristics of a women's approach to theology is the overcoming of some of the dichotomies that have affected theology for centuries. Perhaps it is precisely because their approach is through the concrete, that is, through unity and not distinctions. Scholastic thought, which has dominated theology, proceeds by distinction. Distinction is no doubt necessary at a certain stage in thought, but when distinction becomes the principal concern, we unavoidably become involved in dichotomies. Perhaps a women's approach is more concrete and comprehensive.

I am thinking specifically about the question of justification, where we suffer under a basic dichotomy that is reflected in all our discussions. What is the dichotomy between God's initiative and human action? The question arises from the concern to attribute to each what corresponds to it, and to attribute exclusively, that is, what is attributed to one cannot be attributed to the other. And since in theology we must attribute everything to God we must then in some way or another take everything away from human beings. If we really think from a feminine perspective, if we think comprehensively, starting from unity and not separation, then love is more important than rational understanding, and we start from the basic fact of the relationship of God with human beings. Our starting point is not difference or distinction, but relationship. What is most important is to know what happens in this relationship, and not to whom the different elements of the relationship should be attributed.

I imagine that a theology of justification in a feminine perspective would have as its starting point the relationship of God with human beings, a relationship that generates a dynamic of love pervading all of reality, the whole universe. This relationship comes before the distinction between the justice of God and human justice, between initiative and response. It's possible that at a later point we need to get into the distinctions. But I'm more and more convinced that we have posed the problem backwards and so, perhaps, have not only distorted reality, but have also distorted the biblical perspective. In the Bible the starting point is an action of God in which the people are involved. Human beings are in a relationship with God, a covenant, if you will, where understanding even carnal, physical knowledge, is assimilated into love.

Elsa: Míguez, can't we say that when you are making this effort to re-read justification by faith from a women's perspective, what you are doing is rather a more complete theology, not a feminist theology, but a theology that by including the feminine dimension complements a more masculine theology. Would you agree?

Míguez: Of course. I believe that in the last analysis we are not going to have a masculine theology and a feminine theology.

Elsa: But isn't our present theology incomplete?

Míguez: It is clear that our present theology is incomplete. It is incomplete because there are subjects who have been excluded from theology, not only women, but also the people, particular races, particular classes, whose experiences of faith and of reality have been excluded from reflection. Theological reflection has been not only a reflection of males, but of males situated in a particular place in society, namely, the clerical state, in a particular social class that has usually been linked with the ruling classes. And this has determined their concept of power, of love, of life, and the result has been a deficient theology, a defective theology. Perhaps we are for the first time approaching the possibility of a theology that is really the result of the participation of all the actors of faith and that can reflect this diversity.

Elsa: That's why I think it's important to promote the reading of the Bible from a women's perspective. Otherwise we miss certain things that we should see and that would help us to have a more complete reading of the Bible. The Bible in itself is problematic because it was written in a patriarchal context, but even so we can discover certain liberating elements for women. What is your opinion on the question of the Bible and women?

Míguez: I think that we must start from the fact that the Bible was written in certain historical circumstances, within a social structure where women had particular roles and men other roles; it was a patriarchal society. So I think it's unnecessary and a little annoying to be continuously looking in the Bible for places where women appear in subordinate positions. Because you're always going to find them. You're going to find them everywhere because this was the social structure and the ideology of the people who wrote the Bible and who lived that experience.

I think it's much more useful to find the points where in some way the liberating acts of God are reflected in events, in phrases, in texts, in sudden flashes. Points that break apart in a small way the total predominance of the structure of the oppression of women, and of others as well. That is, the places where we find atypical things happening. And I think these places exist and those who are sensitive to them will find them, namely, women. I already mentioned your reference to "brother and sister" in your reading of James.* I had never noticed this and I know of no one else who had either. Another example is the story of Hagar. I can recall only two presentations of Hagar that have impressed me as significant theological readings of the episode.

---

*Míguez is referring to my study of James, *Santiago: una lectura de la epístola* (San José, Costa Rica: DEI, 1986), p. 42, forthcoming in English from Meyer-Stone Books as *Faith Without Works Is Dead: The Scandalous Message of James.*

One is yours and the other is that of the North American Phyllis Trible, who has a slightly different interpretation.

I think that in the case of the poor the need for such a re-reading is much more obvious than in the case of women. But even so I think the task is worthwhile. On the other hand I think that the distinction, which is sometimes made so sharply, between finding in the text what we are looking for and accepting the text as it is, is a distinction that can be deceptive. Nobody finds in the text what they are not looking for, whether they know what they are looking for or not. And I think it's preferable that women, or blacks, or the poor know with what questions they approach the text and are aware of what they are looking for. Otherwise we are controlled by the questions that the prevailing ideology would have us ask. So we have every right to a controlled exegesis, not simply self-serving, but controlled, with questions that flow from our experience.

To speak in a slightly heretical way — and I feel more and more heretical on this point — I do not think that we can consider revelation as closed. If by closure to revelation we mean that in the mystery of Jesus Christ all is contained, very well. But that is not closure. The mystery of Jesus Christ is a mystery of openness of the love of God, and revelation is not closed as long as we continue to experience the redeeming presence of Jesus Christ. And when this presence enters into a new sphere of human existence and opens it up from within, as in the case of women's experience, or the experience of a particular race that begins to ponder its faith, then revelation is made manifest. No mere literal or conceptual harmonization of perspectives is enough; we have to go to a much deeper level of relationships. I think there is a place for a reading of Scripture from this perspective. In this case it is from the perspective of a sex, but it could also be from the perspective, for example, of a region, or a social group, or the like.

Elsa: Thank you very much, Míguez.

Enrique Dussel

Mexico City, February 1986

We had agreed to meet at 8:00 a.m. at the Hotel Geneve for breakfast of some "ranchero"-style eggs. When he arrived Enrique gave me as a gift a book he had written some years ago, Liberación de la mujer y erótica latinoamericana (Women's Liberation and Latin American Eroticism). We had little time since Enrique was very busy with the committee preparing for a meeting of the Ecumenical Association of Third World Theologians. I was doing the same with representatives from Africa and Asia in preparation for a meeting of Third World women theologians to be held before the general meeting. So in the midst of the confusion of the hotel lobby Enrique suggested we begin and see what we could come up with. By then it was after 8:30.

Elsa: Tell me something about your experience as a married lay person and how it relates to women's oppression.

Enrique: I'd like to tell you how reflection on women's oppression began in my community in Mendoza, Argentina. Around 1969 there was a group of very intelligent and active women. They established an institute called "Social and Family Action," and they prepared a presentation on the theme of "family" for the pastoral agents of the archdiocese of Mendoza. Curiously enough, in our group we began to read Simone Beauvoir and

Margaret Randall. The group was really made up of petty bourgeois: professors, former leaders of Catholic Action; it was a very
aware group. We addressed women's issues very forcefully, both
as a community and as individual couples.

That's where I learned. Often when I had to give a presentation on some theme, I first brought it up in the group for
critique. Gradually I became more sensitive to these issues. For
the first time I discovered that women were indeed very alienated on many levels of real life, social life, political life, life on
every level. We were able to see it in everyday events and even
in crises in marriages where women were becoming more aware
and the men sometimes had trouble accepting it. It was really
very difficult to achieve equality in our everyday lives. Crises
occurred, and there was one separation. I realized that the question was much more profound than we might think, and it is not
easy to resolve.

The alienation is all the greater among the poorer classes
where women often carry the burden of responsibility for caring
for the children and even for their support. But it also exists
among the wealthy. Especially here in Mexico, it's almost accepted for a man to have a mistress in his *"casa chica,"* his
"little house," while under the double standard women are expected to be faithful. At all levels of society in Latin America,
and elsewhere, women are dominated.

Elsa: How do you see women in the church today? Do you
think church structures are unjust? What do you think of the
participation of women in the basic Christian communities in
Latin America?

Enrique: The church is so male chauvinist that we can't even
find documents of the great councils or synods that, for example,
forbid women from being priests or say that a woman cannot
be pope. It's so obvious that these things can't happen that
it doesn't even have to be mentioned. But it's interesting that
since it's left unsaid, this also leaves the door open.

Male chauvinism has deep roots. The Indo-European world

was profoundly male chauvinist, with its father-gods Zeus and
Jupiter. It was a subculture of shepherds or nomads or warrior-
horsemen who dominated women. We see this in Greek philosophy and in our theology. Although the Hebrews gave women a
higher position, men still predominated in their desert society,
so that they called God Father, as did Jesus himself. So from
the very beginnings of Christianity there have been problems. In
the church women have been able to hold only secondary places.
And when there have been great women like St. Catherine of
Siena, they have been known for their prophetic and critical
positions rather than for their institutional or ministerial roles.

So women are faced not with a tradition of two thousand
years, but of three or four thousand, or even more, that they
have to overcome. I don't think it's at all impossible that women
should hold any position in the church. And as I've said before,
in the future we will see women priests, women bishops, and even
a woman pope. The only objection I see is one having to do with
productivity. Women could not do certain things because they
were almost always pregnant. In former periods from the age
of sixteen or seventeen to forty-five or so women were almost
always having children, since infant mortality was so high. So
from a technological point of view women were an economic,
political, and military liability. In those times women were not
able to exercise any moral, political, or religious authority.

There are certain matriarchal cultures, like in Africa, where
women are truly priestesses, but it is usually in the agricultural cultures where women are strong. In general, throughout
the entire Euro-Asiatic world, and even in Africa, nomads over-
came the agricultural peoples. In Latin America, the Aztecs
worshipped the sun-god Huitzilopochtli. They conquered the
farmers. And Tonanzintla, Tonanzin, our "mamma," was the
earth mother who was also dominated. That's why we find the
Virgin of Guadalupe, as a feminine representation of a people
dominated by the Aztecs, who had a masculine god. It is interesting that the Incas also celebrated Pachacamac, the great
god of heaven, and Inti, the great secondary sun-god — both of

whom are masculine. The great cultures organized themselves around the warriors and the nomadic invaders.

So it was very difficult for women to have any political, social, or even religious authority. This means that in some way the church had to mimic the social order to have a hierarchy internal to the church. Women could never play important roles in the church because they weren't able to do so in society. All this is changing very quickly because women are now pregnant for a relatively short period of their lives. Moreover, physical strength is no longer important. In our technological society intelligence is much more important than brute physical labor. Robotization will take this a giant step further. From a technological point of view women are practically equal to men. This allows for economic equality as well as political equality, and religious equality will surely follow. Now we'll need to overcome certain mythical taboos totally determined by history.

Elsa: Speaking of history, as a historian do you think it is possible to interpret history from a women's perspective?

Enrique: Yes, I think you can. Just as you can interpret history from the viewpoint of the poor. It is very difficult, but I think somebody needs to do it, because only by doing it will we see how it's done, right? I think this will be more difficult than interpreting history from the perspective of the poor.

The difficulty is always to find the documents of the oppressed, because the ones who produce the documents are the oppressors. In the criminal archives we discover that an Indian was mistreated, and there we find a document of the poor. History is based on facts. And for doing this kind of history there are certain privileged archives. Here, for example, we have been working with the criminological archives and the archives of the Inquisition.

Elsa: Didn't many women die in the Inquisition?

Enrique: That's one part of it, but here in Latin America in the criminological sector it's prostitution that is especially important. What a curious, obscure, and ignoble place we have to go to study women, don't you think? But it is interesting because we see how the women reacted, how the men reacted, who was declared guilty and how.

There is a basic fact about the history of attitudes and ideas, that is, to produce a women's history means to produce a total history, because in fact every act has been influenced in some way by a mother, a sister, a daughter, a nun.

There are, of course, some outstanding figures, ones who suffered very severely from machismo, because they were aware and fought against it. There is the well-known case of Sor Juana Inés de la Cruz, which I think will gain even more in importance. I think she has worldwide significance as a woman who became aware of women's dignity and confronted men face-to-face. There were few women in the seventeenth century who did this. So I think it is possible to interpret history from a women's perspective; it is difficult, but it has to be done.

Elsa: I've heard you say on several occasions that we must reformulate the concept of masculinity. What do you mean by this?

Enrique: When I first addressed the question of women's liberation, the issue of the liberation of children and the poor came up at the same time. Even in the Code of Hammurabi, it says, "I have done justice to the orphan, to the widow, and to the poor." The question of the widow was very important to me from the beginning. The widow is the wife of the dead other. So she is not my wife but "the other." To do justice to the widow is not even to do justice to my wife. To do justice to my wife is like doing justice to myself. But to the wife of the other, that is true exteriority, love, love of neighbor.

The group of three — orphan, widow, poor — appears in all the prophets and in Jesus as well. And Bartolomé de las Casas speaks of it too: "The Spaniards arrived and reduced the indigenous peoples to the most horrible servitude, leaving only the children and the women alive." The women were their mistresses. So we soon discover that the mother of Latin America is the mestizo mother, the Indian. And the father is not the Indian but the Spaniard. So the Indian woman was very important for me. What was your question again?

Elsa: About the need to reformulate the concept of masculinity.

Enrique: Ah, yes. I recall the words of a psychologist, Francisco Sosa, who said, and this was over fourteen years ago, "If women are liberated and assert themselves, they are going to have to re-educate the men, they are really going to have to redefine them, because men will have no identity." A male chauvinist identity is very clearly defined. When a man sees his partner begin to assert herself, he begins to founder, he no longer knows how to define his masculinity. So the problem is how to redefine masculinity. We have to re-educate men on how to be men.

We don't really know what it means to be woman, since it's only now being discovered, and so neither do we know psychologically, pedagogically, ecclesiastically, or in many other ways what it means to be a man. This gives rise to a new theme, the redefinition of the man. And it means the death of a certain kind of couple, the death of the male chauvinist family, and the birth of a family of equals, where the woman asserts herself and the man has to be redefined.

This is an extremely interesting subject that is going to become increasingly important, when the women who have gained self-confidence themselves provide the reference point for the redefinition of men in the society of the future. We cannot say this about the present society, for this is not something that happens in one generation; unfortunately it takes many. Sometimes a woman who has begun to be liberated finds it difficult to transmit her sense of struggle to her own daughter; the environment is so strong that the daughter is reared in anti-feminist values. Then there is the generation that struggles for women's liberation, the second generation that accepts it as natural. And it's possible that in a third generation women will finally be equal to men who have been re-educated in families where the mothers are liberated. The theme is complex.

Elsa: In Latin American theology women are increasingly the subjects of theological discourse. To the degree that women do theology, with a women's consciousness, we think that their theological discourse could offer some new angles. This is not really a question of producing a feminist discourse, but of helping to complement Latin American theological discourse from a women's viewpoint, by contributing other dimensions. What do you think?

Enrique: Women have the great advantage of being sensitive to theological questions, which they handle quite naturally. Only women can truly make the contribution from this perspective. I don't think that men can contribute any more on these issues, but have to study them as outsiders. And as I've said men have to study the redefinition of masculinity itself.

At this point it's the women theologians who have to address these topics and have to show us how to discover them. And if theology can be completely rethought from the point of view of the feminine face of God, then it is women who will be able to discover the feminine face of creation and of history, of the church and of everything else. Women have to take the lead so that we can see what will be produced. Then we can take up these themes again. I think that this is the moment to give the floor to women theologians so that we can develop this thorough revision of theology from a feminine perspective.

I believe it's somewhat analogous to what we were saying about the theology of liberation. The theology of liberation is not a chapter of theology but rather it's all of theology considered from the viewpoint of the poor. Theology from a women's perspective is likewise all of theology seen from this perspective. Because we can look at God, the Trinity, christology, ecclesiology, the sacraments, all of exegesis, all of history. It's truly a total revision.

It's interesting that some people think that this hasn't been done before. But from, let us say, the second century when Alexandrian theology appeared, every generation has started over with theology from its own point of view. And this is the history of theology, that is, we can't say that it's a new idea for us to want to revise theology, for that's a most natural step. We can revise all of theology from the perspective of the oppressed. Women, as part of the oppressed, are going to revise theology from a women's perspective, so that in the next generation Christian women are going to find themselves perfectly defined, clarified, and affirmed in a Christian tradition revised and renewed from their point of view. This is a very basic element in the liberation of women.

Elsa: Let's speak for a moment about women religious in Latin America. In the Catholic church religion is potentially a great power. Various studies have confirmed this. Would you agree?

Enrique: From the very beginning of IPLA (Latin American Pastoral Institute), there were many women religious in the courses that were presented. This is also true of the courses given at CLAR (Latin American Confederation of Religious) in Bogotá. In Latin America there were more than 140,000 women religious consecrated to the gospel. Of those 140,000, it seems to me, there were very few who were dedicated to truly prophetic tasks, that is, the tasks of church renewal and service to the poor. Because of a spurious mysticism, many of them were alienated to a nonexistent man, because, as I understand it, they often thought of themselves as the brides of Christ. By establishing such a relationship to a man they were projecting the machismo of society onto Jesus, and they were transformed into women dominated by a nonexistent man. This is quite serious. On the other hand, if religious consecration were considered to be a self-giving to others, that is, to be a companion of Jesus as the twelve apostles were, then these 140,000 women would be transformed into a truly explosive force, for no other organization has 140,000 "full-timers" working for the gospel.

Nonetheless, it is the women religious who have really renewed the Latin American church, for they are very much more sensitive to poverty; they have an enormous capability to embrace poverty. By the very fact that they have been raised in a male chauvinist society, they have been trained for service. So they are more attentive to others than anyone and are willing to undertake situations of greater risk. They are the greatest prophets on the continent. The congregations of women religious are the ones that have renewed themselves after Vatican II, after Medellín, and it is they who in fact are carrying the prophetic church, the poor church forward.

Paradoxically, those who have not kept up with renewal remain profoundly alienated within a male chauvinist church, but those who manage to renew themselves are the most positive elements in the church today.

I think another theme we must study very much in depth is mysticism. From the contemplatives of the third and fourth centuries up to Teresa of Avila and even Thérèse of Lisieux, we need to study this spirituality. Women's issues are also involved here, including the question of the domination of women.

So we have to move from this level to the level of concrete commitment. I really think that this is one of the most important topics for discussion among women religious in Latin America.

Elsa: Enrique, tell us something about your personal life with your family.

Enrique: I believe I've had an advantage. During the sixties I was in Germany. I was married, I had a scholarship, and I was doing my thesis on the history of the church. What happened was this. My wife was working as a schoolteacher, and I had to take care of our son. I watched after him in the mornings, and she in the afternoons. I think the father's participation in the raising of the children is very important, especially when the woman is also a breadwinner. My wife was never dependent on me, whether economically, or in her work, or in her self-fulfillment. The two of us shared economic and psychological responsibility, as well as the task of rearing our children, at least for the long time that we were out of Latin America. She has always worked, and so have I.

For me it has been a tremendous help to know that my wife could always support the family if I were fired from the university. So my wife has always been the one who has insisted on the liberation of women with me. She has not allowed things that a lot of other wives allow. Of course we have had arguments and confrontations, but I owe to her the fact that I not only discovered these topics, but that I have also established a relationship with my partner that is quite different from the norm with regard to participation and the raising of the children. Remember that in the mornings I had to feed our baby, I had to change his diapers, I had to put him in his play area. I was writing my dissertation and he was playing. And when my wife returned he was quite content in his carriage. He was waiting for his mother. But I had been with him from seven in the morning to one in the afternoon.

These experiences helped me to discover many levels of life. When the theme of women's liberation came up, for me it wasn't new but rather had been very important since the beginning of my marriage. My wife educated me in this matter. But we have to recognize that the environment is very powerful and machismo is very widespread, so it's easier to go along with things as they are. When we get home it's so easy to fall into the routine of the wife preparing dinner and the husband reading the newspaper. This is what happens every day, and it's what we have to overcome.

Elsa: Thank you very much, Enrique.

Rubem Alves

Geneva, Switzerland, May 1986

I interviewed Rubem three days after I met him for the first time, although we had been in contact through our writings and correspondence. We were each having breakfast alone in the John Knox dining room at the World Council of Churches. From his table he said, "Good morning" to me, and I answered, "Good morning." He asked in English if I had come to the 450th anniversary celebration of Calvin, and I answered that no, I had come for a meeting of the Programme for Theological Education (PTE). He asked my name and where I was from. When I told him, he said, "I'm Rubem Alves," and he joined me at the table. We shared an abrazo, and I soon realized that he is as crazy as his recent books suggest. Three days later we had the interview in the comfortable chairs of the John Knox lobby. It was about 10 at night or in the morning; I don't recall which.

Elsa: Rubem, is women's oppression in Latin America a reality or not?

Rubem: The problem with this question is that the answer can be banal if we just say that, yes, oppression is real. I think that first of all we have to distinguish between women. When we speak of Latin American women, whom are we talking about? There are peasant women, working-class women, middle-class

women, upper-class women. To answer the question in a mean-
ingful way and not with a banal "yes, oppression exists," we have
to see clearly the faces of the women we are talking about. The
oppressions that women suffer are very different. In some cases
the "oppressions" are accepted, because they pay dividends.

There are oppressions that can work to your advantage. In
certain cases women are the accomplices of their own oppression.
So for the answer to be intelligent we would need something like
an exposition of pictures of the faces of Latin American women.
Then we would see the precise nature of each oppression on the
face of each woman.

Elsa: How would you describe the situation of women in the
Protestant church?

Rubem: Very ugly.

Elsa: Women or the church...?

Rubem: Both. The situation of the church and the situation
of women both look ugly to me. In the case of the Protestant
churches, especially the Reformed churches, it's terrible to see
how women were — I don't want to say desexualized — were led
to lose their sensuality in the broadest sense of the term by
virtue of a religious ideology.

What we often see in the Protestant churches is women quite
impoverished as women. Our religious ideology is repressive of
sex, and women are not allowed to be women. It is women who
define themselves as mothers, and not only as mothers, but also
as wives.

In the blessing of the traditional wedding ceremony it doesn't
say that woman was taken from man's head to be superior to
him, or from his feet to be tread upon and oppressed by him,
but that she was taken from his side, from alongside his heart to
be his companion, from beneath his arm to be protected by him.
So you always see the idea of companion, of complementarity.
The idea of woman as a separate entity, beautiful in herself,
autonomous, mistress of her body and of her life, is not the

usual image. Women's groups in the Presbyterian church are
even called women's auxiliaries.

Who are women in the church? Women prepare the lunch
for visitors. Women are always there, helping out in one way or
another. But they are absent. So I don't see a beautiful place for
women, unless you consider the place that women have now to
be beautiful, and there are some who do. If you define women's
function in this way, you will accept the image of woman as
mother. And the image of mother is a beautiful one: the Pietà
is beautiful. Catholic theology has an image of the Pietà that
is a combination of mother and lover. Because she is not the
mother of Jesus; she's too young for that. She is mother and
lover. This is the drama of Oedipus. In our images we don't
have anything similar that relates the figure of mother with the
figure of the woman who loves. Well, we do have Mother's Day.

Elsa: But that's something cultural.

Rubem: It's cultural, but it's also terrible, because it's the day
that brings out all the aggressive feelings of the children. The
problem is this: anybody who doesn't have an ideal mother to
love, as beautiful as the Pietà, is condemned to contend with
real-life mothers. And when you have to contend with real,
concrete mothers, then you are forced to idealize them. Because
Mother's Day idealizes our real mothers: mothers are wonderful.
The feelings of aggression become inescapable, because we all
know that mothers aren't what we say they are on Mother's
Day. It would be interesting to do a study on the feminine
images that we have in Protestant discourse. One of the worst
for me is that of Mother's Day. You said that it's cultural, but
it is very much a part of Brazilian Protestantism.

Elsa: But Mother's Day is a commemoration by the whole of
society, not just the churches. Do you see any hope for change?

Rubem: I'm speaking of the churches that I know best, those
of the Reformed tradition, and to be perfectly honest, I'm very
sceptical. I don't see many signs of hope. And I'm not speaking

just about the image of women. In the Reformed churches it has to do with everything, the images of women, of men, of society, of theology. They are churches that have become petrified.

Elsa: How would you like the church to be?

Rubem: Calvin used an expression that I like very much. He spoke about a *pia conspiratio. Conspiratio* means to breathe together. So the church is basically a community of persons who con-spire, who breathe together as one, with the same desire. It is a community of desires. In *The City of God,* Augustine says that a people is defined by the object of its desire. If we want to use more modern terms, we can speak of the erotic. It is a community that celebrates the same erotic objective. Erotic in the sense that... And it's precisely this, do you know what I mean? That celebration of what is desired, of the erotic. For God's Reign to be desired it has to be erotic. And this is what I feel is lacking in the church. That's why the church doesn't get me very excited. The church that I love is not an empirical entity; it's rather an object of my dreams. I dream of a church, and that's why I stay connected to it.

Elsa: You've written about the question of inclusive language. In Latin America we still have a long way to go in this area, but it's becoming an issue. What do you think about inclusive language?

Rubem: It's true that our language excludes women — in its grammatical forms. When concordances are compiled, they always are based on the masculine form. There is a whole range of mechanisms by which women are excluded from the language. God is male. Women have become aware that language usage is a trap and that this systematic exclusion of the feminine was not accidental, but rather a way to define women's identity, a way to define the world. Then women began to insist on so-called inclusive language, that is, language in which women are always present. When we speak of God, we should say He/She. Women should never be excluded. I wrote an article against this idea. I don't like it. First, because it's ugly; it's not beautiful; stylistically it is very ugly. And anything ugly doesn't arouse love in anybody. It might even be true, but nobody becomes passionate about it. I can't become passionate about a God who is he and she at the same time. I get very confused. If God is he and she, then God is a hermaphrodite.

My feelings as a human being are separate. When I love a man, I have love for a man (my father, my son, my friends). I also love women (my daughter, my wife, other women, my students). But these are different loves. If I mix them up, I get very confused. So my objection is that that language disturbs me erotically.

I think that theological language is a language that should express the pulse of desire. Sometimes I desire a woman, and when my desire is for a woman, then God is a woman. Only a woman. There is no reason to put a man in the middle. Sometimes my desire is for a man — a friend, a son — and when my desire is for a man God is a man. You don't have to put a woman in the middle. Sometimes my desire is for neither a man nor a woman, but for a tree, for the moon, for the sea, for silence, for fire, for water. When my desire is for those things, then God doesn't have to be either man or woman.

What I'm trying to say is that the name of God is a mystery that embraces the whole world. And since I cannot speak of the entire world within this mystery, the only thing that I can say is the name of the desire that I feel at any given moment. This means that I am really never speaking about God. I don't know who God is. God is just a name for my desire.

I think that inclusive language is a language of generalities, for when you have he and she together you have neither he nor she. This is the theological equivalent of what Marx denounced in economic language, namely, the passage from use value to exchange value. For example, with use value, if I have a violin, an orange, and a cow, they are not interchangeable; each is absolutely unique. When I desire a violin, it's only the violin that I desire; it's not a cow. When I want a cow, it's only the cow I want, not the orange. Money is the inclusive language of economics.

Military people also use inclusive language. When they say "the enemy," they include children, old people, men, women. Military language is a language that deals only with inclusive entities.

I have a feeling that this movement for inclusive language is part of a movement in our civilization that is quite repressive. So I'd like to see us return to absolute specificity in the language of desire. When my desire is for an orange, it is an orange I want; when it's for a violin, it's a violin I want; when it's for a woman, it's a woman I want; when it's for a man, it's a man I want; when it's for the wind, it's the wind I want. Poetic language, theological language, at least in my opinion, is not a language of generalities, but the language of absolute specificity that appears in poetic language.

Elsa: But this doesn't mean that it's denotative par excellence.

Rubem: What do you mean by that?

Elsa: When you say, "I want an orange, and it's an orange that I want," that's clear denotation. But theological discourse and especially poetic discourse is highly connotative. You know this very well since you're a poet yourself.

Rubem: Ah, yes! But that's what I was about to say. The interesting thing is that the Christian God is the God of the incarnation, which can be translated in this way: the absolutely universal becomes absolutely concrete. I work with universals in theological language, by employing very concrete images. And when I speak in theology, I use very concrete images. For example, bread, an extremely concrete image, is not only bread. It is symbolic, parabolic, metaphorical. It is a network of assembled relationships. The problem with inclusive language is that in order to be inclusive it empties out the sensuous content.

Elsa: Let's move on to another subject, your new way of doing theology. You include a ludic perspective, play, pleasure. How does this affect the theme of women or women themselves. Have you thought about this?

Rubem: I've never thought about how it affects women. But I will say this that I think this model of doing theology is an erotic model. I no longer work with the category of truth. I don't know what truth is. But I know what is beautiful, I know what is good, I know what gives pleasure. I think that bodies are moved not by a conviction about truth, but by the seduction of the beautiful. I am developing this theology because I am interested in seeing people do things. And a theology based on epistemology, no matter how fierce, doesn't move people. We are not constructed in a Cartesian way. We are erotically constructed. I don't know if this affects women, but my theology is affected by women.

My model for doing theology is an erotic model; it is a sexual model for doing theology. Because what happens in sexual experience is that each participant is a playful plaything. At the same time that I am the woman's plaything, without feeling that I am being used, I am also playing with her. This is the symbol of pleasure, of what we do with no sense of usefulness. But just as in sexual play a child can be born, a child can also be born of theology. Something can happen. How that affects women I don't know, but I think it is affected by feminine images.... No, I won't say images, because as soon as you say feminine image you have to think also of its counterpart. You have to think of the masculine image. You can't think of the feminine image by itself. When you think of a feminine image, you have to think of the corresponding masculine image.

Elsa: I have a problem: Who decides what is beautiful, what is good? Torturers get pleasure from torturing.

Rubem: For me that's the point where faith comes in, for faith means that I have criteria for distinguishing one pleasure from another. You know that I work in psychoanalysis. Psychoanalysis is a pessimistic doctrine. It was through psychoanalysis that I began to recover the Calvinist meaning of double predestination. I always thought the idea of double predestination was horrifying. After I began reading psychoanalysis, I thought, "Maybe that crazy Calvin had a point." Because psychoanalysis says that we are all a mixture of life and death, of *eros* and *thanatos,* and this *eros* and *thanatos* are not democratically distributed. Some people receive an abundance of life and little death; others receive a lot of death and little life. Psychoanalysis has no explanation for this. It simply observes it. Some people have an absolutely incredible will to live. They endure the most horrible experiences and they survive. But others are in situations that objectively are more normal and tolerable, but there is an internal power of destruction that destroys them. They commit suicide.

So the fundamental question is to identify where the pleasure is that is related to life. I would say, for example, that the function of preaching is to be able to exorcize death and invoke life. The same is true for theology; it's a question of discerning spirits. We have to be capable of discovering the pleasure that leads to life. Is it where we are working or not?

So in relation to your question, it's not just a matter of pleasure in itself. It seems that the first pleasure of the child is the pleasure of the womb, the experience of the womb. Two things occur together there: nourishment and pleasure. It is not only nourishment, nor is it only pleasure. It is nourishment and pleasure. It is life and pleasure. The task of theology is something like this. When we do theology we have to be capable of recreating an experience of pleasure and life at the same time.

Elsa: Thank you very much, Rubem.

Carlos Mesters

São Paulo, Brazil, June 1986

When I asked Carlos Mesters for an interview, he said no, because, he said, his mind goes blank in front of a microphone and he doesn't know how to give long speeches. I told him I didn't believe him, that he had to demonstrate this for me with a microphone in his hand if he wanted me to believe him. Besides he has had a lot of experience with basic Christian communities, and what I was looking for wasn't a speech but to hear about his experience with the women in the communities. So we went to his room, and he said that when he couldn't come up with anything that I should interrupt and ask him something else. I said that that would be fine. That's how this lovely interview came about. When we were finished we went to have a drink with our friends, also Scripture scholars. It was about 10 p.m.

Elsa: Carlos, on the basis of your experience with the basic communities or with the poor, how do you see the oppression of women. Do you think that women are really oppressed because they are women?

Carlos: Women's whole experience, for example in the backlands that I know in the Brazilian northeast, and in many other places, is one of true oppression. Women have no voice; they exist to work; they hardly speak; their place is in the kitchen.

They have a child every year. They are pregnant all year, and in the meantime they have to take care of the children. Their husbands often have to leave, to go to the south to work, and the women remain alone at home. The burden is so great, the oppression is so great, that we can't help but wonder if there is any way out. Oppression is very great, especially in the backlands, which I know a little bit about.

The culture itself is responsible; it's not that a particular individual is oppressing women because they are women. The culture itself is male chauvinist. When a girl is born, a father will often say, "What a shame! It's a girl. If we had only had a boy." It seems that girls aren't as important because they don't carry the family name. Males carry the name. Women receive the name of the men they marry, so they're in second place. That's what I've observed.

Elsa: Among the people, in the movements of the poor classes, what does women's participation look like?

Carlos: Women participate very much. But I want to say something else about your first question. Once I was speaking with a woman named Antonieta. I mention her because she is like a symbol. She was very oppressed by her father. So she thought, "I'm going to find myself a husband," thinking that by getting married she would be free of her father's domination. So she looked to marriage for liberation. But marriage was like prison for her. Her husband was worse than her father. She had a son and thought, "My son will liberate me." But her son went south and left her alone. So this woman was a daughter without a father, a wife without a husband, a mother without a son. Antonieta said to me, "If it weren't for God, I wouldn't love anyone, if it weren't for God. But I love them all." Her attitude was a symbol for me. In spite of all the oppression, Antonieta kept going. I felt about this big in her presence.

Elsa: Tiny.

Carlos: Yes.

Elsa: So women do have strength.

Carlos: A lot of strength, a lot of strength. Where it comes from I don't know. It's a bottomless spring that always gives water.

You asked me about the communities. Most of the people who participate in the communities are women. They bear the burden of the daily work in the communities. Within the communities of Brazil a movement is being born of women who have begun to realize that they have a voice, and this is part of their new self-consciousness as women. I don't know much about the feminist movement, but from what I can see the women's consciousness movement here is not against husbands. They want to be partners and to struggle together for the greater liberation of everyone. They want to have their place in the liberation process. And so in many places their struggle has a very wide scope. It is not restricted to their own liberation; this is a very hopeful sign. The movement is still small, but it exists in the communities.

Elsa: While we're speaking of the basic Christian communities, how do you see the relationship between women and the church? Traditionally the church has been very male chauvinist, patriarchal. Wouldn't you agree?

Carlos: It doesn't matter if I agree or not, it's a fact. It's a fact that the church has always been run by men and has always been very male, always.

Let me see if I can make myself clear. Men themselves are hurt by a macho culture. Not only are women hurt, but men too. To the degree that women manage to struggle for their own space, they liberate men as well. I think that this is very good. I don't know a lot about psychology, but from what I've heard, within every human being, there are both masculine and feminine elements. The masculine exists in women and the feminine exists in men. And the feminine is repressed in both. And it should be reborn and regain its space and be expressed concretely. I think that the space is still very small within the church. In the communities the people are making progress, but there is very little in the official church.

Elsa: And how are women making progress in the basic communities?

Carlos: They are speaking up. And when they speak, people listen. I think it's very important for people to be able to speak, and be listened to, for when they are listened to it's a sign that what they are saying is important. It's very simple at first. It involves listening to what people say, remembering their names, trying to remember their names, since their mother and father gave them their names and they will have their names for the rest of their lives. It involves remembering each person's story, which for that person is very important. In the communities the women — and the men as well — are reappropriating their own stories, their own names. Someone thinks they are important, and they are becoming persons, because of the gospel.

The fact that they are loved by God is expressed concretely when they are loved by each other. This is happening in the communities. And women play a very important role, because they perceive things that male eyes don't perceive. Little things that allow the free communication of the human word to flow more easily in the community. And where the human word circulates freely, the word of God produces freedom. So women are a factor that allows this to happen in a lot of places. Of course we also find the opposite; there are people who dominate. But I'm speaking in general terms of what I have seen.

Elsa: Speaking of the Bible, you have done a lot of work with the Bible in the basic communities. Do you feel, do you think, that women can read the Bible with different eyes than men?

Carlos: You asked two questions, first, whether I feel this, and, second, whether I think it. I'd have to say that I still don't feel it, but I do think it. I think that there should be women exegetes, interpreters of Scripture. Reading the word of God as women they are going to discover things that male exegetes have not discovered, because behind their eyes there are things that men don't have. And the more they take the word into their own hands, the more they will discover. A black woman said to me, "I am a poor, black woman, but when I speak, my word is a bullet." As women become aware of their situation their raised consciousness becomes a new light in their eyes that sees in the text things that men cannot see. I believe this, but I have not experienced it enough to feel it. I hope and pray that it will happen.

Elsa: Can you recall some examples that make you think ...

Carlos: Once I was at a meeting of women religious who live and work with the poor. They came together to reflect on the Bible. The theme was prayer, and the meeting lasted three days. We weren't sure how to begin. We made a *mutirão** to find in the Bible passages that speak of women praying. I was amazed to see how many passages our *mutirão* produced. Then we asked another question: For you, women today, what are the characteristics of women's prayers in the Bible? And a third: Do you recognize yourself in these texts, in these prayers? It was a very rich and beautiful experience. And there was a kind of connaturality between what women experience today, their suffering, and what they saw in the Bible.

We also have had meetings with men and women together; it seems good to me to have both together. Then it's more difficult to say what comes from the men and what from the women, because our interpretations are a community task. They don't come from a single man or woman.

Elsa: Carlos, what have you learned from women?

Carlos: I've learned a lot. It's difficult to say. First we learn from our mothers, right? We shouldn't forget that. Then we learn from our sisters and from our friends. We learn from their attitudes, their resistance, their patience, and their hope. We

---

*Portuguese expression meaning a project done together through teamwork, like a traditional house-raising or quilting bee.

find people who have children, create children, produce children in extreme poverty, and for me that's an act of faith in life, an act of hope, an act of total dedication. I learn from that. I'm not married, but I don't think I have as much faith in life, that kind of commitment, that kind of hope. I've learned a lot from all that and ... It's difficult to answer. I'd need some time to think about your question.

Elsa: One last question about the Bible, and especially hermeneutics. How can we approach the Bible, a book written in a macho culture. Do you have some guidelines?

Carlos: I don't have a lot to say about that. It's a difficult question. I think of the sixth commandment, which we often translate as "Thou shalt not sin against chastity," but in the Bible it says, "Thou shalt not commit adultery." I think that chapter was written to attack the root of oppression, which is the domination of women by men. When the Bible says not to commit adultery, it makes no distinction between men and women. It's the same for both and so takes men's privileges away. The reality was there, for men always had privileges, but the ideal was that God made human beings in the divine image and likeness, and so God made men and women equal.

Jesus adopted this ideal and said to Peter, "Anyone who looks at a woman lustfully commits adultery." Again he took away men's privileges and established equality. When Peter realized this he said, "Then it's better not to get married." And I think it would be better if a male chauvinist Peter didn't get married. If he is going to get married with a male chauvinist mentality, it's better that he not get married. I think Jesus was very demanding. I don't think Jesus' words are moralistic; his idea is to affirm equality, to say that men no longer have privileges. That's the main point: Jesus takes up the initial ideal, the human being made in the image and likeness of God; that's why God made us man and woman.

Then the Bible recounts the pilgrimage of a people that tried to achieve the ideal, but didn't. They weren't able to practice the sixth commandment, that is, they weren't able to achieve the objective, which is to pull out oppression by its roots. This is the basis for totalitarian systems, namely, the domination of women by men. I think that this is the underlying support for political systems that oppress people. Would you agree, Elsa?

Elsa: Yes, I think so.

Carlos: One of the deepest roots of totalitarian political systems is to foster the small family unit, where there is a pyramid with the man over the woman and both over the children. And if we can manage to create freedom there, to break the relationships of domination that spread through the communities, we plant a very subversive seed within society. But we haven't achieved this, nor did St. Paul. Paul says, "There is neither male nor female in the community," but he also said, "Women shouldn't speak in church." The practice was less than the ideal. And it's the same today. It's a shame, a shame. It should be different. Perhaps the basic communities are a sign of hope.

Elsa: Don't you think that there's something women can do as we become part of the liberation project?

Carlos: I think that Latin America can do a lot. I think the women of Latin America are present. Here and there something new is happening.

Milton Schwantes

São Paulo, Brazil, June 1986

It took us awhile to decide where to have the interview. The campus of the Methodist university where we were staying was very noisy, and we didn't have much time. The meeting of Scripture scholars had ended, and Milton was leaving for São Leopoldo. We decided to go to the house of one of the professors and talk on his patio. We got two chairs and began our conversation. After the second question we decided to move because of the noise and the sun. At the meeting I had noticed Milton's enthusiasm for analyzing the Bible on the basis of modes of production. The same enthusiasm is apparent in his ideas about women. I asked him to speak in Spanish to make my task easier, and he did so very well. It was about 9:30.

Elsa: Milton, do you think that the oppression of women is a reality in Latin America, or is it just the latest imported fad?

Milton: You ask if women's oppression occurs in Latin America. Yes, you can see it everywhere. I don't think the answer is the generic assertion that, yes, there is oppression, but rather we need to identify it concretely and to analyze its origin. There is oppression; it's clearly visible. In a very general, phenomenological sense we see that violence against women is quite severe and permeates all classes of society, every sector, the working class and other classes as well. Violence against women, and also against children, is very serious. In Brazil there has just been introduced a special police force to protect women. Women can call to report men who have beaten or raped them. The police discovered something that people didn't know, that not only in the lower classes but in the middle and upper class as well physical violence against women is very serious. You don't read much about this in the newspaper.

In Brazilian society black women are the typical domestic employees. This work in some ways is a continuation of slavery, because they work in people's houses, they don't have any social security, and they are very directly dependent on the people they work for. This is a very clear case of oppression. We also find oppression among indigenous women, peasant women, working women. Women are oppressed with regard to salaries; they are paid less. Indigenous women have been oppressed since the time of the conquest and the invasion of Latin America. So there are many groups of women who suffer violence and oppression.

An important question, and it seems to me best that women work it through, is how this violence, so clearly visible, should be interpreted. There must be many reasons for it. One interpretation is that this violence is very closely related to the exploitative capitalist system in Latin America. This system doesn't touch everybody in the same way. Everybody is unequal. Equality occurs only among those who sell for capital. Otherwise, everybody is unequal, and some are more unequal than others. Children are discriminated against more than adults, young people more than older people, women more than men, and so on.

There is a whole hierarchy of inequality, and in this hierarchy women are very oppressed. But there's another question, which is not so closely related to the problem of class, and that's the institution of marriage. It's very surprising to see that among young people (and this is not only recently, but has been going on for several decades) there now exists the possibility of equality between young men and young women. But it seems to me that the institution of matrimony is one of the very typical spaces of oppression of women. At the moment women enter into marriage, the institution itself requires their submission. Before marriage there is some space for freedom, very carefully controlled of course, but space nonetheless — at least, say, in the middle class. But as soon as women are married there is a commitment to subjugation.

We should analyze, especially in the church where the institution of marriage is so strong, how strengthening this institution is perhaps providing a privileged, eternal place for subjugation. There's much more to be said about this, because I think it's very typical of the poor and middle class. Marriage is a capitalist mini-enterprise, and in a capitalist mini-enterprise, all the roles are roles of subjugation.

Elsa: Speaking of the church, Milton, how do you see women's participation in the Lutheran church?

Milton: In the Lutheran church, we see something of the same system that we find in society in general, that is, the church repeats much of what exists in society. The Lutheran church in Brazil is somewhat special, in part because of its origin in European immigration. Although that's not so important now, it is important to remember that its members were originally small farmers who were able to produce autonomously. They had their own space because they had a small piece of land and could produce on it.

Under these special circumstances the Lutheran church had certain cultural characteristics. (This is not so much the case now, because most of the people don't have any land and live on the outskirts of the cities.) Women had a position with a certain amount of autonomy because they had a very active role in production. Peasant women work together with the men to make the land productive. This gives them a dignity that comes from participation in the management of the product made in the countryside.

Women's participation is reflected to some degree in the church, for in the church women participate especially at a community level. In the community, in worship, in things related to the home, women are relatively strong. But when we leave the home, leave the house to go into banking or business, that is, into an area beyond the farmer's land, beyond the family's house, women's participation is almost nonexistent. Men appropriate the socio-economic relationships outside the home. This is reflected very clearly in the church, for on the most representative levels of the church, the regional and national levels, participation is almost exclusively male. This is the way it's been traditionally.

At this moment women in the church are the ones who are best organized. There are groups of women in the communities who are very well organized and participate very actively there. We don't see this reflected in overall church structures. There are almost no women represented on a regional level, and the few that we do find are quite isolated. Nonetheless, there are new kinds of pastoral programs. The younger pastors, both men and women, who take a grassroots educational approach, are developing programs for consciousness-raising, that is, programs where there is gradually created a space for women outside the community within the people's struggles, for example, for land or for adequate public transport.

So we are finding more women in the struggle for land, participating in strikes. In the church it's still a minority involved in this kind of thing. There are some, but they are a minority.

Elsa: As a Scripture scholar, tell us about your reading of the Bible with the basic Christian communities. How do women read the Bible? And another question having to do with hermeneutics: How should we approach the Bible, a book written in a patriarchal society?

Milton: Your first question is about women's reading of the Bible in the communities.

Elsa: Yes. Have you noticed any special contribution made by women in their reading of the Bible in the communities?

Milton: Yes, let me see...

Elsa: In your own experience.

Milton: In the congregation the difference in readings between men and women seems very clear to me. In my experience women's readings tend to be more concrete. When women are part of a Bible group, they bring things to the Bible that are closer to life. Men have a tendency to generalize, to bring in elements from wider arenas of concepts, like politics, for example. But in my experience women's perception is more sensitive to little things, exact things, concrete things. There is a difference between men's reading and women's reading; their perceptions are different.

Nonetheless, we also have to remember that women, in many cases, tend to repeat the prevailing ideological values of society, that is, a male perspective. This is not rare, but happens quite often. Sometimes women speak in a more sexist way than men, because they reflect the prevailing ideology of a society that belongs to men. Among the women pastors or other pastoral agents, the differences are more developed, more explicit, clearer, because the people involved in pastoral activity generally are more accustomed to self-criticism, to an understanding of what is happening in society on an ideological level. There I have seen very clear examples of different readings by men and women.

Now I think we can move on to the second point, to the exegetical and hermeneutical question. I want to distinguish the two because in hermeneutics we try to get beyond this oppressive ideology, which is dominated by men, and approach a text to re-read it from the perspective of the poorest. Because of their historical experience of oppression, women are able to be more in tune with the biblical testimony from the perspective of the poor. I have seen very clear and classic examples of women's ability to perceive in a text the perspective of the poor. That is feminist hermeneutics, a hermeneutics from the perspective of the poor.

I'm a member of a group where we are going through this

exercise. We have a group in Porto Alegre that has been meeting for two years. We are trying to verify how the poor classes on the outskirts of the city and in the countryside read the biblical testimony, how poor women read it. And how from the same perspective we might read the testimony of Scripture on an exegetical level, that is, on a little more technical level.

So the poor, oppressed women of Brazil, struggling for liberation in the countryside and the city, become the hermeneutical key for re-reading the text. This brings to light many important things in the Bible that haven't been seen before. It also brings to light the oppression of women in the Bible itself. In other words, the Bible goes from being a sacred text to a guiding witness expressed in a language that we don't like so much today. So there is a perception of the Bible as a voice of the poor, and there is a perception that in the Bible there is also the voice of persons who are against the poor, especially against women.

Then comes the more exegetical part. Here I have some questions about what I have read on the question of women in the Bible. We more or less presuppose that the Bible was composed by men, and I think that this supposition is questionable. We have this impression (and it's a historical question) because in Judaism and in the history of the church it has always been men who have read the Scripture. The history of interpretation gives us the impression that the Bible was written by men. In fact, men's participation was very important, but I think we have to ask if this conclusion corresponds to the historical facts. Historical research is required.

The Bible was written in a society whose mode of production was completely different from the modes of production that we know in the West, that is, the slave system, the feudal system, and the capitalist system. As we know these systems are defined basically by men. Under these modes of production women do not have a significant role in social decision making. The question is whether we can transfer this model to the tributary mode of production that we find in the Bible. And that's where I have my doubts, because the tributary mode of production is characteristic of peasant society. Under this mode of production the peasants are the strongest element, and ideologically the most decisive element, in society.

We know that among peasants in a tributary system women have a very significant role. Peasant women have three principal spaces. First, they have an important space for the rearing of the children; this is the space for reproduction. Second, they are involved in production in the countryside. And, third, they have a role in the distribution of food. So in a tributary society three basic social realities pass through the hands of women, and this provides a very important social and political space for them.

The Bible was written under this system of production, in which women had a very important role. Now we have to ask, which sector produced the Bible? Under the tributary system there is the peasant sector and the urban sector. In the Asiatic mode of production, women in the cities are oppressed. We see this very clearly in Solomon, the harem, the cows of Bashan (Amos 4:1), and in other texts. Women were dependent and oppressed in the city. Did the biblical texts originate in the city where men play the dominant role, the exclusively dominant role? I don't think so. Some of the biblical texts come from that situation, but very few, relatively very few.

It's possible to think that the creation of the whole Bible, its origin, is to be found in the peasant sector. I think that this is the case, that the Bible comes from peasant culture. If it does, it seems quite clear that Jesus, the prophets, Abraham, and the Hebrews in general come from that sector. And the psalms of lamentation all come from the peasants.

If it is true that the peasant sector is the hegemonic sector in the creation of Scripture, then we have to ask whether women's voices are important in Scripture. There are texts in Scripture that come from the voice of women. They may have been written by men, that is possible, but they give every indication of representing the interests and the culture of women. I don't think that this research has yet been carried out, because we haven't asked whether under the mode of production we find in the Bible the text might have its origin with women.

I think there are many texts that come from women. The book of Ruth speaks of women, but is it not also a book created by women? What are the criteria for distinguishing a book created by a man from a book created by a woman? Is the Gospel of John written by men or by women? And I'm not referring just to the technical question of writing, but to the intellectual question. In the ancient world writing is not synonymous with intelligence. For us it is the same, but it wasn't then. In the ancient world intelligence didn't depend on writing: Socrates was very intelligent but he didn't write anything. Jesus was an intellectual in that tributary world, but he didn't write anything. Creative intelligence was not necessarily identified with the act of writing.

So it seems to me that we have a lot of work to do in two areas. First, there is hermeneutics, that is, what does a particular text (which may even have been written by a man) mean for women? The apostle Paul wrote texts. How do we read Paul from a women's perspective? I think there are other accents, other discoveries, other critiques of Paul that men are not going to see. Paul says that women should be silent in church. Throughout church history, this has hardly ever presented a problem to male exegetes. It becomes problematic from a women's perspective; there is a change of perspective.

The other question is the exegetical-historical one. We have to ask again where the Bible comes from, from what world of peasants, of men, of women. I think there are many biblical texts that come from women's culture.

Elsa: Thank you very much, Milton.

Frei Betto

São Paulo, Brazil, June 1986

To be honest, our interview was somewhat forced. If it hadn't been for Betto's considerable experience in answering questions, I don't think anything would have come of it. The atmosphere wasn't conducive to an interview. During my brief stay in Brazil I had only a few minutes to talk to Betto, and it wasn't women that we wanted to talk about. Josismo, a priest who worked in a rural pastoral program, had recently been murdered for his defense of peasant rights. That night I met Betto in the cathedral at the six o'clock Mass. In the church was a cross draped with the bloodied white shirt of Josismo. Cardinal Arns preached from the altar surrounded by posters demanding justice. Frei Betto wore his white Dominican habit. After Mass we had our interview under a street lamp on the campus of the Methodist university. It was about 10 at night.

Elsa: Frei Betto, speaking from your own experience, do you think the oppression of women in Latin America is a reality?

Frei Betto: Yes, it's especially apparent on a continent like Latin America. Here women suffer oppression both at work and at home. Women are victims of the ideological oppression reflected in the culture we breathe. and in a certain way women help continue the oppression insofar as they, as mothers, teach

91

their sons the traditional "division" between masculine and feminine that is imposed by society: boys shouldn't play with dolls or play in the kitchen. In our churches women are nearly always considered second-class citizens, the ones who do the less important jobs. In the home women take care of the living utensils; in the church they take care of the utensils used in worship.

This is all crystallized in the profound identification that exists between the relationships of production and the relationships of reproduction, which both have the same oppressive character. The reproductive relationships between a man and a woman reflect the contradictions between capital and labor in the relationships of capitalistic production. Sexuality comes to have a commercial character, whether it's the mere reproduction of persons and labor in the family, or the unjust use of women's labor, as if women were by their very nature less qualified than men.

In this way the entire dimension of intrinsic otherness is lost to the love relationship and, therefore, to pleasure as an expression of gratuitousness in the giving-of-self-to-other. Women become mothers relegated to the home, while men feel that they have the right to look for pleasure in extramarital relationships. Here I'm speaking of pleasure as belonging to the realm of fantasy, of aesthetic recreation, of the way life is perceived. I'm speaking of the sexual encounter transfigured into liturgy which, from a theological point of view — as recounted in the Song of Songs — expresses the mystical union with God or the encounter of Yahweh with the people. The "pragmatism" of maternity is the death of the wife-lover and of the relationship of loving gratuitousness.

There are two countries in Latin America that are trying to break this macho cycle: Cuba and Nicaragua. But centuries-old roots still influence the behavior of both men and women. The process of women's emancipation threatens the hegemony of the masculine, which is surprised in its natural insecurity (for we still have the mistaken notion that men are more secure than women). Men react aggressively. Their aggression is against women, for they cannot bear for women to demonstrate greater intelligence, to be better educated, or to earn higher pay than men. Their aggression is against themselves, as some prefer to marginalize women and seek their *alter ego* in homosexual relationships. And their aggression is against society, as they practice a sexual liberalism in the name of a supposed transcendence of a repressive morality.

In capitalist as well as socialist societies the division between the public and the private spheres prevails in men-women relationships. Privacy, including sexual privacy, is a personal question that reflects a political context.

To ignore this principle leads to contradictions and ambiguous behavior, like the theoretician who publicly proclaims anti-macho concepts and at home practices the vilest oppression of his own partner. Only a profound reflection on the ethical and moral questions involved in political activity in general, with their consequences for the private sphere, will allow the veil to fall; because the veil is transparent it cannot hide the contradictions.

Elsa: Let's talk a little about the church. What is your opinion of the church's relationship to women?

Frei Betto: In the Catholic church, at least in the traditional structures, women continue to be second-class citizens or "minors." They can't be deaconesses, priests, or bishops, and they are allowed to work only under male supervision — even if they are superiors of an order or a religious congregation. In the Protestant churches they can be pastors, or clergy, as in some Anglican churches. They are able to preach and even to fill leadership positions. I suppose there are more Protestant women theologians than Catholic...

Elsa: I'm not so sure about that. But in the basic communities, how do women participate there?

Frei Betto: In the basic Christian communities, where we see a new church arising from the people, women play the same roles as men. I very much like Augustine's definition that "the church is an old woman pregnant with herself." In the womb of the old church, where the new church is being born, women are the protagonists in every ecclesial activity and creation. In many of the basic communities of Brazil where there are no priests, women lead the worship, interpret the word of God, organize the celebrations, etc. When men participate in the community, they understand the role their wives are playing. But when the men are not part of the community, they get jealous and put obstacles in the way of their wives' activities.

Domestic relationships of male supremacy are socially reproduced. The men feel threatened by the intelligence of their partners, for it is ideologically understood that men are "the head" and women "the body." Two heads are intolerable, at least from a male perspective. But when the couples participate together in the communities, where these themes are frequently discussed, these "values" are changed, and there is a better understanding that machismo is a reflection of the domination intrinsic to the capitalist relationships of reproduction.

Elsa: Betto, how do you see the participation and the contribution of women in the grassroots movements? Is there something special about women's contributions?

Frei Betto: I don't think so. In the grassroots movements women have the same role as men, whether in neighborhood movements, in protest movements, or in solidarity movements. I think that Latin American civil society is divided into five spheres: the pastoral area, the grassroots movements, specific grassroots movements (women, blacks, indigenous peoples), the labor movements, and the political parties. In all these areas women have been gaining a role of great importance allowing for the full expression of their abilities. The greatest difficulties are probably still in the pastoral area and labor.

Elsa: Frei Betto, what do you think about including in the first act of the theology of liberation the praxis of affection, on the same level as the praxis of justice and spiritual experience?

Perhaps the systematized theological discourse, the second act, would be less rigid, don't you think?

Frei Betto: I think that flexibility in theological discourse is a requirement for both men and women. Theological discourse is a language about God. It is the quest to express the experience of faith in a rational manner. And the experience of faith is fundamentally an affective experience, at least as spiritual initiation to an understanding of the gift revealed in Jesus Christ. In the strictest sense, this mystical experience is beyond the senses and beyond affect. That's where we find the nucleus of our fully human interaction. I think that women are more sensitive to this experience. They are intuitively more open to the gift of the presence of the One who is a closer friend to us than we are to ourselves. Women have a greater ability to link, in their theological work, the heart and the head, feeling and thinking, intuition and rationality.

Elsa: Thank you very much, Betto.

Leonardo Boff

Petrópolis, Brazil, June 1986

I arrived about noon to have lunch at the Franciscan friary where Leonardo lives. After lunch Leonardo showed me where the rest rooms were. They were large, public rest rooms and I said that the seminarians were going to be surprised to see me there (I was the only woman in the place). He replied that he had already warned them that there would be an angel walking around. I said that it was an unusual angel that had to "peepee." Leonardo laughed. We went to his comfortable office for the interview. He asked me if I wanted a drink of some kind of liqueur, and I said I didn't drink. He insisted, saying that it was good for colds. I took a sip that felt like fire in my throat, and I began to cough. We laughed. Then Leonardo opened the window and showed me the mountain. "Isn't it beautiful?" he exclaimed. "Yes," I answered, for indeed it was. It was about 2 p.m.

Elsa: Leonardo, from your own experience how do you see the oppression of women in Latin America?

Leonardo: It seems to me that women are oppressed on almost every level: family, society, church. Our culture, at least in Brazil, is very macho. Women are always considered in relationship and connection to the home. Although women are the bearers of life and the educators, they are not allowed the space to fulfill themselves as human persons. Rather they are always a function of others. They remain invisible even though they are present, because their presence doesn't count in our society.

On the other hand, an awareness of this oppression is growing. In the basic Christian communities, especially, a very important space for the liberation of women has been created. This is not so much because there they deal with the theme of women's liberation, but rather because over half the coordinators of the communities are women. In all the basic communities it's the women who are most engaged in the work. They are more faithful. It is they who guarantee the continuity of the groups, which are usually quite fragile. At first the men don't participate because they say that the communities are "for women." But later, after they begin to participate, they realize that with women as coordinators things work better. There is more tenderness; the atmosphere in the church is less conflictive. In the places where there are communities, women have more strength to deal with problems of hunger, disorganization, all kinds of limits to life. The women are very courageous. They are also very intelligent in organizing the communities and moving them forward.

I also see in the Brazilian church a greater awareness that women should participate at every level, in theological reflection and in many other areas, including pastoral planning. More than thirty-five sisters run parishes; they are already functioning as parish priests. They do everything except consecrate the Eucharist. Their celebrations are very well prepared; the men say that they like the sisters' Masses more than the priests', because they are much livelier. So we have this ambiguity. On the one hand there is the very oppressive macho tradition. On the other there are movements that in fact provide the space for women to take on responsibilities and participate.

In this sense we can speak of dimensions of liberation. But we still need reflection on this practice, for the reflection has only just begun, and the reflection can be done both by male theologians and women themselves. There are women who are organizing, who reflect on their faith, who teach theology. I'm very happy that during my period of silence* when I was unable to teach, a woman theologian, the mother of three children, very competently filled in for me and was very well accepted by the students. She was able to combine all the depth that a feminine perspective provides with the seriousness and objectivity of her understanding.

Elsa: Leonardo, I would like you to speak a little about black women. As you know, black women and poor women suffer the greatest oppression in Latin America, and here in Brazil the percentage of the population that is black is very high.

Leonardo: Yes, in Brazil we have some forty million blacks. Brazil is one of the largest black countries in the world. In 1852 more than half the population were black slaves. The blacks were the only ones who worked, even though today they are often considered lazy. They built this country by their slave labor. Black women were always the family servants. In my family two black women helped my mother with her eleven children. From my earliest childhood I personally had a very deep relationship with blacks because two black women helped in rearing us. Black women are very oppressed and poor, but they are present at every level of white society. They are domestic employees and help raise the children. So there is an interactive presence of blacks, but it is always in a subordinated form, unrecognized, almost like an extension of slavery.

On the other hand in the Afro-Brazilian religions over 70 percent of the centers for ritual are directed by women; this has been demonstrated by anthropological studies. And this, I think, confirms what has been pointed out by many anthropologists, namely, that women in general are much more sensitive to the sacred, the profound, the mysterious. They are the mediators of this dimension of Afro-Brazilian religion, which is very closely linked to mysticism, which in turn is very closely linked

---

*Leonardo is referring to the "silence" imposed on him by the Vatican in 1985.

to the body, to dance, to ritual meals, to the basic structures of life.

So I think that the position of black women is very contradictory. Personally I don't see it very clearly. On the one hand they are enslaved and marginalized. On the other they rear white children; they hold the children in their arms, they guide them and educate them. So the racism that does indeed exist in Brazil does not appear so visibly as it does in the United States. Here it is more internalized. If you are white and from the upper middle class, you have had one or two black women in your home. We have been accustomed to seeing them there since we were children. But they were always subordinates, employees, the ones who had to do all the work. And they were very tender, very affectionate with the children. The situation of black women is very ambiguous in Brazil. They are exploited, but at the same time they are something like the mistresses of society, but the mistresses of the unconscious, of the children's early years.

I'm not exactly sure how this is structured, but I see a problem here. I'm not sure how to analyze it. It reminds me of how Greek culture was dominated by the Romans but ended up conquering Roman culture. This is typically Brazilian. We see the contributions of blacks in Brazilian cuisine, music, rhythms, a very deep religious sensibility. In all this we see the black contribution to Brazilian culture. Now these contributions are shared by all, but the assimilation was mediated by blacks, and by black women in particular.

Elsa: You have already mentioned the very important participation of women in the basic communities. Could you say something about women and the church as such, and their future?

Leonardo: I would say, almost in jest, that no matter how much we are threatened by nuclear war and the destruction of the earth, none of this will occur until the church rectifies its historical sin of marginalizing women from the very earliest centuries until today. The church is basically a church of males, a church of whites, and a church of celibates. Women are present (since they obviously reproduce persons who are Christians). But women are almost invisible on the level of church structures, decision making, church law, pastoral planning. My slightly utopian vision is to imagine that the third millennium will be the millennium of the Holy Spirit, who is more and more breaking into human consciousness. It is the Spirit who takes what is of Christ, deepens it, develops it, and assures that the Good News of Jesus is permanently "Good News." At the same time the Holy Spirit is very closely related to the feminine. *Ruaj* is feminine. The Holy Spirit is linked to life processes, the in-breaking of what is new. The Holy Spirit is not the continuity of the church but the discontinuity that allows for something new.

Now that human experience has become universalized, with the encounters between cultures, the category that allows us to understand the new realities that are breaking through is *pneuma,* the Holy Spirit, its charisms. The task that faces us is to find a wider space for the Spirit that allows for freedom for charisms. And this means a wider space for women, because the Spirit is very close to the vital process of the production of life, the defense of life. It has a different relationship with the world, not one of control, but of tenderness, of welcome. As long as we don't develop this attitude, which is a human attitude, but is more developed among women, I don't think we can get beyond the enormous "ecological" crisis that we've got ourselves into. I think that this is the path ahead for humankind, for I dream of the day when men and women, considered as different but equal, not only as male and female but as human persons, will each contribute their gifts. This will make for a much more balanced society, under the sign of wisdom, of *sophia,* which is the grand archetype, the grand myth; it has a feminine origin but it also has masculine traits, because it is a creature and at the same time it creates playfully, tenderly, affectionately, lovingly.

We are approaching this new era, I think, and are already seeing its first signs. I believe that it will be an era of much more historical balance, with much more meaning to life, respect for life: all that lives deserves to live.

I think that women understand this language better, and so I very much hope that women can take control of the political direction of human destiny that is clearly headed for death, for the non-reproduction of life. This is the great crisis of Europe. Europe has chosen death; couples do not reproduce. I think that women better perceive the meaning of life, its mystery, its dignity, and could direct a less conflictive history, more integrated, more tender, with other forms of life that are more loving.

Elsa: Let us speak now of christology. If you had to write another book on christology, how would you do it from a women's perspective?

Leonardo: I want to mention two points that are important to me in any christology that includes a feminine dimension. First, we need to show that Jesus as a human person developed his feminine dimension, that is, the whole dimension of compassion, of tenderness toward the poor, the marginalized, children, women. We cannot understand this dimension if we don't understand the *anima* within the *animos,* within the masculine. I find Jesus fascinating in this regard, because he was able to integrate this dimension. He is neither macho nor rigid nor violent. He was able to integrate, on the one hand, the clarity of divine power, which does not waver or compromise, with, on the other, tenderness and compassion when he encountered persons in their weakness, in their human situations. And I think that's where we see the feminine dimension of Jesus. We need to develop this further.

Second, we need to look more closely at the relationship between Jesus and the women in his life, particularly Martha and Mary, whom Jesus loved as he loved Lazarus. And we should look closely at Jesus' encounter with Mary Magdalene, who threw herself at his feet, wept, and anointed him with oil. This is a ritual of love, of intimacy, that Jesus confronted publicly. He defended this contact with the woman who touched him, who kissed him. A think we need to read this without any moralizing, we need to integrate the sexual dimension in its deepest meaning into our reading. It is a question of the man-woman relationship, which goes beyond genitality. These texts are extremely rich in showing how Jesus has integrated this profound dimension of the man-woman relationship. It seems very clear to me in the case of Mary Magdalene. Then there are the long dialogues with the Samaritan woman, with the adulteress. Jesus has no prejudices. He sees women not in the first instance as women but as human persons, worthy of respect, worthy of being heard. These are very rich passages; we see that Jesus had no prejudices, whether moral or cultural. We have to look more carefully at this dimension of Jesus, now that we are conscious of it. I have tried to do it here and there in some of my writings, but we need to do it more systematically.

Elsa: It's true; I've noticed that you are one of those who has written most about women. How did you become interested in this question?

Leonardo: I come from a family of eleven, with six sisters. So from the time I was a child I have had profound encounters with women, both within my family and with friends at school. For men, women are always an abyss, a mystery, a question. From an early age I asked myself how feminine destiny fits into the divine plan. The Bible says that we are the image and likeness of God only as man and woman together; how then does the feminine reveal God? How is God revealed in the womb? For me it was not so much a question of Mary or women in the church, but rather of the feminine dimension that exists in all of us.

Anthropology tells us that the feminine dimension is present in both men and women, but in women it is more visible, better expressed. Church tradition has reflected this very little. We find it more among the mystics, for the mystics break through dogmatic formulas and traditions. They grasp reality as it is. I've always been concerned about this, but I don't think I've reflected or written on it enough. I need to deal with the question in a much more systematic and profound way.

I once had a very privileged personal experience. Standing before the image of the Virgin of Guadalupe in Mexico, I saw hundreds of persons approaching on their knees. I asked a number of them if they adored the Virgin. And they answered, "Father, how could I not adore the Virgin? Of course we adore the Virgin." This virgin is pregnant, and pregnant virgins are few and far between. The person of Jesus is in Mary's womb, and there too is present the Holy Spirit creating the humanity of Jesus at every moment. But at that moment, Mary is, as tradition has always held, "the temple of the divine," "the tabernacle of the Holy Spirit." So at one moment of history, Mary is the center of everything. She is the center of the two divine missions; she receives the Holy Spirit before she receives Jesus and from her feminine humanity the Holy Spirit creates the humanity of the eternal son. At that moment Mary holds within herself both missions, that of the Spirit and that of the Son. And in this sense Mary is the center of humanity.

And so when the people say that they adore the Virgin, they are adoring that complex and comprehensive reality that is unified. For anthropology also tells us that during gestation mother and child are a single reality. They are not two separate realities, but rather a kind of *pericorisis,* one within the other. The humanity of Jesus is the humanity of God, and it was given by Mary. It is a feminine humanity that comes from Mary, and so the feminine is divine. I understood this in a moment of enlightenment there in Mexico, and that is when I began to work on my book that was later entitled "The Feminine Face of God."

Elsa: Leonardo, I want to talk with you now about theological methodology. Do you think that in the first act of the theological task there should be the praxis not only of justice, but also of affection?

Leonardo: Yes, I believe that affection is at the heart of the

option for the poor. We make an option for the poor first of
all because we feel a profound compassion. This doesn't mean
to feel sorry for others (which is to look on them from the outside). Rather it is compassion in the sense of sharing another's
destiny, life, struggles. We can do this only if we have affection,
tenderness toward the poor, sharing in their lives, making their
situation our own. I think that this is part of practice, but we
haven't reflected on it. This might be because men have done
most of the reflecting, and we immediately decode the situation
in an analytical way. We have not appreciated the emotion, the
tenderness, the affection, the cordiality contained in the experience.

I await this important collaboration of women, for they are
humanly better prepared to perceive this reality and to express
it. There is a dimension to our analysis of reality that we must
complete and improve, because in the end what convinces people, moves us to action, are not the analytical considerations,
but the fervor of the heart, the passion for a cause; it is affection,
a very deep, committed love.

For me this has a great theological significance and relevance.
For in the end God is love, not love as an expression of a will
that wants things, but a love related to God's will for good, the
God who is tender toward the poor. And if this God is the God
of hosts, God uses those armies against the oppressor and not
against the people. So I think we need to fill this out. More
than fill it out, we need to filter the entire liberation experience through feminine experience. The feminine experience is
a totality: the way we experience God, grace, Christ, as well
as commitment, courage in the struggle, the force of resistance.
Women do all this in their own way, which is different from the
way men do it.

Throughout the whole theological enterprise there is a tremendous gap that only women can fill. If they do not offer that
collaboration we will be deprived of a greater experience of God,
and a fuller revelation of God will be denied to us. This is the
basis for my criticism of the one-sided expression of the church,

of the church-institution, built upon men and leaving women on the edge. For it does not allow women to tell the church about their experience of God, of Christ, of salvation, of sin. It does not allow them to enrich all of us with their experience and so reveal to us the face of God, which is the face of God the Mother, of the paternal mother or the maternal father.

Elsa: Thank you very much, Leonardo.

Pablo Richard

San José, Costa Rica, August 1986

We had been trying for some time to set aside a moment for an interview. But since we worked together in DEI, we had unintentionally let the time go by almost until the manuscript was ready to be typeset. Pablo is always on the run, as am I. I didn't show up for our first appointment; I forgot. Pablo couldn't make the second because he had a previous engagement that he had forgotten about. Not only did we have trouble coordinating our schedules, but also in arranging for a tape recorder, for when we finally did get together, our recorder didn't work properly at first. We settled into one of the DEI offices that had an electrical outlet. As we talked and sipped coffee, I realized that Pablo had learned a lot from women. It was about 2:30 in the afternoon.

Elsa: Pablo, the first question has to do with women's oppression. Do you think it's real, or is it just the latest fad?

Pablo: I think the oppression of women is an obvious, widespread, profound reality. Women's oppression affects all of reality, not only women, but the economy, politics, society, culture, religion, ideology, church. Women are the principal victims of the oppression, but they aren't the only ones. All of reality in all its dimensions is affected by the oppression of women.

And that is why women's liberation means not only the liberation of women; it also means total liberation. Women give me a vision of the totality, a total worldview that necessarily leads me to the situation of women. I cannot analyze or liberate reality without reference to women. There is an expression of Lukács that I have always liked; he says that the totality is concrete, and maybe that's why women provide that vision of the totality and of concrete reality. I can't think about economic reality in concrete terms if I don't consider it from the perspective of women, who have a direct, immediate relationship with oppression, as well as with liberation, with life, with the reproduction of life. I cannot think about political reality, grassroots reality, ideological reality, if I don't have women's reality very clearly in mind.

I think that a women's worldview helps us complete our vision of reality. I would compare it to the worldview of culture, of race, and of religion. These are other concepts of the totality. The concept of culture includes all of reality. The concept of religion embraces all of reality.

I think it's been fatal for the Latin American Left to hold to the Marxist idea that the man-woman contradiction is secondary, or to consider the problems of race or culture as secondary contradictions. By relativizing women's issues, by relegating them to a secondary position, we lose not only the women's dimension but also a sense of reality, a sense of the totality. So whenever there is a grassroots struggle, an economic struggle, an ideological struggle, or any kind of struggle and women participate, just as when blacks participate, that struggle truly takes on its own identity, its own concreteness.

If women's liberation isn't part of it, it is as if the struggle were abstract. Women provide the dimension of concreteness, of totality, of identity, and also provide us with the capacity to resist, to struggle. To give a concrete example, I've always been impressed by the mothers of the missing persons, the disappeared and detained, particularly the mothers who marched in the Plaza de Mayo in Argentina. Why do we always hear about

the mothers? Aren't there fathers too who suffer as much as
the mothers when their sons or daughters disappear? I think
we hear about the mothers precisely because of their capacity
for struggle and resistance. These demonstrations on behalf of
the disappeared have turned into a nightmare for the system,
of course, because these women looking for their children are
relentless, they do not quit. Men give up very quickly. When
men see that something is impossible, they quickly say, "We
know that they're dead. This is absurd. They've disappeared
because they're dead. We're never going to get an answer." But
the women don't quit.

We see the same thing among the poor classes. Men often
run from reality, saying that they're going to look for a job in
another town, in another city, in another country. Women have
that ability to resist precisely because they are so closely linked
to concrete reality.

Women make us discover the poor, the poor as they really
are. We often speak of the poor, but they can be nothing more
than an abstraction. When women speak of the poor, they take
on a very concrete, vital meaning. It's the same for children.
The concept of the child also leads me to the totality, to concrete reality, to discover the concrete meaning of the poor. By
the same token, the poor have led us to discover the reality of
women.

So for me it's very difficult to separate the concept of the
poor from the reality of women. One leads to the other. This is
especially true in Latin America, where the struggle for women's
liberation is not a struggle against men but against machismo. I
think this is fundamental in Latin America. Machismo oppresses
men as much as it does women. It is a total reality; it is not
partial, it is not secondary. Machismo dominates everything,
culture, ideology, the economy, politics, the political parties, the
church. That's why the struggle for women's liberation takes on
a total character, for the enemy is total.

There is a dimension of machismo that I want to stress,
machismo in politics. Politics in Latin America, politics with

a capital P, that is, participation in the public arena, has been exceedingly male chauvinist. Why? Because the taking of power has been emphasized. I think that this obsession with power has a very macho connotation. Women's participation has shown us another dimension to politics: the "what for." I'm not saying that this is more important, but it is just as important as the taking of power. I'm not saying that the taking of power is male chauvinist, but to unilaterally exaggerate power is.

This other dimension of power, power for what, has been lacking, that is, power to build what kind of society. This has to do with the whole utopian, transcendent dimension, the description, the enjoyment of the new society. I think that this has "de-machoized" politics. It has been precisely women's participation that has raised the political questions from a different perspective. But let's move on to the second question.

Elsa: The second question has to do with women in the church. What can you say about the present situation?

Pablo: As you know, one of the ideas I've dealt with a lot in my writing is the opposition between Christendom and the church of the poor. I think that all of Christendom, as a model of the church, has a direct relationship with the exercise of power. Christendom is a power structure, it is a church that uses power as a mediation to assure the presence of the church in society. And I also think — and here I'm using an ecclesiological key — that Christendom is a macho structure. That is, Christendom has been continuously dominated by men. The feminine figure does not appear and is not even able to appear. It is even difficult to imagine a feminine figure, a woman in Christendom.

But this is not the case in the church of the poor, which is the model opposed to Christendom. In the church of the poor the structure is not one of power but is rather communitarian. Women have been able to participate in the church of the poor, and at the same time women's participation has led us to discover a new model of the church because of that affinity between women and community experience. Women's participation in the church is extremely important if we are to move from Christendom to a model of the church of the poor.

In the second place, one of the characteristics of the basic Christian communities is its creativity, which stems from concrete reality, and this doesn't happen without the participation of women. I've really seen this in my own experience. When women actively participate in a basic Christian community it is much more creative.

I also think that the question of women's ordination is fundamental. We won't move from Christendom to a church of the poor if we don't have women's ordination on all levels. We cannot exclude any level, whether that of priesthood, deaconate, or episcopate. I see no theological reason for the exclusion of women. But we have to address how this ordination will come about, because if women are ordained as priests, deacons, or bishops within a Christendom model, women will be destroyed — unless this ordination accelerates the transition from Christendom to the church of the poor. And I think that women's ordination will be the signal that the transition is being accelerated. We must ordain women; the higher the position and the quicker it is done the better. But this struggle has to take place within a broader struggle, which is the struggle to move from a Christendom model to a church of the poor.

There's an important dimension in the church that many theologians have pointed out, that is, the passion for Mary that the people have. I don't think that this is just a cultural or a Catholic phenomenon. There is a deeper substratum. At the basis of the cult of Mary there is a protest against the image of a macho God. God seems too authoritarian, too overpowering. Mary represents the feminine character of transcendence. She is an accessible, concrete, human, maternal transcendence. I think that in popular Marian piety there is a protest against a macho God and the search for a different God.

Elsa: Pablo, if a women's perspective is incorporated into traditional theological discourse, will it make a difference?

Pablo: Yes, I think that when women do theology it brings a totally new dimension, because women do theology — as all theology is done — on the basis of their own experience of God, their own spirituality. I've always been impressed by the statement in feminist theology that "God is she."

If women do theology on the basis of a spirituality that expresses their experience of God, their own reality, this radicalizes tremendously the method of the theology of liberation, because the starting point is truly a totally different experience of God. It is different from the spirituality that has informed all of theology, exegesis, christology, the theological, historical, and philosophical tracts.

Western culture is totally impregnated with a concept of God that is foreign to reality. So when women do theology not only do they bring to it a new theme, a new dimension. There is something more; they challenge all of theology, the whole Western intellectual enterprise. It seems to me that women's theological task breaks much more radically with the prevailing theological models than does theology done from the perspective of the poor. Because in the last analysis the system has a great ability to integrate the poor as part of the system. The poor are generated by the system, while women make us discover "the other" within the system.

So women challenge, I would even say destroy, the classical theological method and radicalize the method of the theology of liberation.

Elsa: Pablo, have you learned anything from women?

Pablo: To speak personally, my relationships with women have made me discover the negative side of being a man. Being a man means having an attitude of control and pride, a consequence of the control and pride of society. Men are very lonely. I think women are less lonely than men. (This is only a hypothesis since I'm not a woman.) But I'm speaking of the loneliness of men that stems from their pride and their desire to dominate. Women have helped me personally to overcome this desire to control. When I speak of the desire to control I'm not speaking so much in the political sense, but rather of control through knowledge, through opinion, through reasoning, through writing. And this necessarily leads to a position of pride. Women have allowed me to leave my isolation, to get beyond this desire to control.

I think it is very difficult for men to be humble and sociable without a relationship to women. Women get men out of their isolation, their pride, their power, and finally they allow men to get beyond themselves and to become humble. It is the man-woman relationship that humanizes. There are theologians, church leaders, priests, bishops, and men in general who are tremendously dehumanized. I'm not saying they have to get married to become human, though that would be one concrete possibility. A relationship with women is fundamental, both for married and for celibate men. I believe that the humanization of men is very difficult without this relationship.

Human beings are meant to be helpful, humble, sociable, communicative. I can't imagine a celibate theologian, a celibate priest, who could be fully human without a very profound relationship with a woman. We can even see this in the great saints, in St. Francis of Assisi, in St. John of the Cross, in Jesus himself. I think that Jesus' relationship with women was very deep, very essential. Women have a powerful influence over men. This might be a considerable heresy, but it's something that I've experienced personally.

Elsa: Now you're getting into trouble.

Pablo: For me this is basic. A man who is unable to have a relationship with a woman is never going to be able to leave behind his attitude of control, his pride.

Elsa: Let's move on now to the Bible. As a Scripture scholar, Pablo, you know that women are trying to find new hermeneutical guidelines from a women's perspective. I'd like to know your opinion about the possibility of such a hermeneutics.

Pablo: In the first place, I think that women's participation
has enabled us to find new dimensions of the Bible that we did
not appreciate in all their depth and beauty and intensity, for
example, biblical figures like Deborah, Anna, Judith, Ruth, Esther, the mother of the Maccabees, and many others, including
Hagar, whom you discuss in your article.* We didn't appreciate these figures before. It was as if they were marginal to
the Bible, always subordinate to masculine characters. If we
read the Bible from the perspective of these women, we really
discover a different Bible. I've always been impressed, for example, by Esther, with her great capacity for fidelity to her people.
Many have called her the historical memory of the people. This
is a dimension of revelation that we hadn't discovered before.

In the New Testament women's participation is extraordinary, especially in the Gospels. In Mark 14 there are two meals,
one is the meal in Bethany and the other is the Last Supper. We
always hear about the Last Supper, but the supper in Bethany,
where the woman pours perfume on Jesus, could be much more
important than the Last Supper. At Bethany we see a relationship with the body of Jesus, and Jesus feels that his body is
being prepared for burial.

Jesus' gesture of recognition that his body was being prepared for burial has a foundational character for the Eucharist
as great as his words "This is my body that shall be handed
over for you." But since it is a woman, who in the text itself
is looked down upon, the apostles are concerned only about the
price of the perfume and not about her; but the woman is worth
much more than the perfume.

Jesus' attitude toward the woman's action is remarkable. He
says that her action is important, because the perfume is being

---

*Elsa Tamez, "The Woman Who Complicated the History of Salva-
tion," in *New Eyes for Reading: Biblical and Theological Reflections by Women
from the Third World,* ed. John S. Pobee and Bärbel von Wartenberg-Potter
(Geneva: World Council of Churches, 1986; Oak Park, Ill.: Meyer-Stone
Books, 1987), pp. 5–17.

poured out on a poor person, Jesus, by another poor person, the woman.

Reading the gospel from a women's perspective gives us another view. Women, for example, were witnesses at the foot of the cross, and women looked on the crucifixion from afar. Later when Jesus was buried the women saw where they laid him. And women were the first witnesses to the Resurrection. We know that in that period women were legally unable to be witnesses, but for the early community, they were indeed privileged witnesses. The second part of the book of Revelation is filled with women, for example, the woman clothed with the sun with the moon under her feet in chapter 12. Rome as prostitute and the New Jerusalem as the spouse of the Lamb are others. There is a whole range of feminine symbols in Revelation that is totally overlooked by exegetes.

If we read the Bible from this perspective, we read it differently, because there is a male way of reading the Bible. You speak about this in your article, "La fuerza del desnudo" (The Power of Nakedness). What is this male, I'd even say macho, way of reading the Bible? It has to do with control of the truth, wanting to control the truth. But there is a different way to read the Bible, to discern the truth in reality. I would call it a feminine way of reading the Bible. Women are much more capable of discernment while men are more capable of control, that is, men have been trained to control. This would be an exegesis that does not try to control the truth, but rather one that tries to discern the truth, the word of God in reality. In this sense exegesis from a women's perspective, and even more, exegesis done by women, not only uncovers new themes in the Bible, but also provides a new way to read the Bible, one characterized more by discernment than control.

Elsa: Thank you very much, Pablo.

Raúl Vidales

Mexico City, August 1986

I went to Mexico City twice, but didn't have the chance to interview Raúl. On my first visit I had no time, and the second I had no heart for it: I saw him at my mother's funeral. I decided to ask him the questions over the phone, and he responded with the following letter:

Quito
4:50 a.m.

Maruja and the children are in Peru, so I can't sleep at night. I tried to write several times, but I couldn't get anything down on paper.

Since I'm leaving tomorrow I did my best to come up with something as spontaneous as possible. I'm sending it to you just as it came from my head. In any case I've written it from the bottom of my heart. Please try to adjust what I've written to your four questions, since I've answered only three. Or just leave it as it is.

Greetings to Duque, love to your two precious little devils. Maruja, the children, and I send you our love.

Raúl

Elsa: Raúl, what do you think about the oppression of women in Latin America? Tell us something about your own experience.

Raúl: To tell you the truth, I didn't expect this question, but

115

I'm glad you asked it. After the earthquake in Mexico City women appeared on the social and political scene playing many important roles in organization, mobilization, and leadership. This phenomenon certainly wasn't a miracle of the earthquake, but it undoubtedly helped speed up the gestation process. In any case the old saying was reconfirmed: "Only chaos gives birth to a star."

I've been thinking about these things for years, first, within a political practice directly oriented to the organization and mobilization of women in poor areas on the outskirts of the city. Many of the struggles for vital necessities, housing, food, medicine, schools, wouldn't have had the relative success they did without women's participation. But I also remember the expression of an old utopian socialist, "The degree of women's emancipation is a natural measure of universal emancipation." Or in the words of one of the geniuses of the contemporary liberation movement: "The proletariat cannot achieve full liberation until women's liberation is complete." Historically there has been a social division of labor between the sexes, just as there has been private property and social classes. Juridico-political structures guarantee control of one social class by another. The oppression of women continues to be reproduced in these structures of exploitation that are increasingly subtle and effective.

Let me mention one example. It is absolutely necessary for imperialism to maintain and foster the various forms of oppression of women in the dependent countries. The division of labor according to sex that obliges women to take care of the household is fundamental to capitalism. In the heart of the individual family, labor power is privately produced and reproduced in the multiplicity of continual everyday tasks that women exercise. These are not recognized socially, but capital appropriates their surplus value. Domestic work has been reduced to a merely biological reality, even though it is basically economic.

We have to encourage what Agnes Heller calls "the revolution of everyday life." This is one of the subversive elements that takes on a great explosive potential as imperialism becomes increasingly impotent not only to satisfy basic necessities, but also to guarantee them and not attack them. For aggression exists not only in strategic geographical locations but at the heart of everyday life itself.

In our social system women have a clear role assigned in "private life," but if they want to venture out into "public life" they have to enter into the marketplace. But ordinary, everyday life acts as a cell for ideological and cultural reproduction. Here, of course, religion and its structures play an important role. This is where the struggle for minimum subsistence becomes explosive. Among the poorer classes, it is more and more difficult for women to provide a human level of basic necessities for their families. So the struggle for minimal subsistence is part of both everyday struggle as well as the political projects in which many women are engaged in our countries.

What is new is not only their political consciousness, but also their organization and mobilization in programs for the building of new societies. For a long time we didn't realize it, but there has been both a qualitative and quantitative multiplication of the "Domitilas," the "Jovitas," the "Mamma Tingos," the "Tomasas." There are now exemplary women's political organizations in Chile, Argentina, Central America, Mexico, the Caribbean. We have to look at the concrete steps, the real-life experiences, the particular struggles that by their profound nature transcend any merely anecdotal consideration. In this way we will discover the specific characteristics of the feminine face in the process of building new societies.

Elsa: Do you think women's participation is important in theological production?

Raúl: Since the answer is so obvious it can fool us. Of course women are real subjects of and in theological-biblical production. But I'd like to mention a few points that, I think, complicate the enterprise. Women are in a radical way producers of theology, whether in their everyday lives or in decisive moments of a process. They express the creativity of the faith of the people, their unitary vision of life. They demand the right to work, to bread, to housing, to health care, but these struggles are joined to uncontainable explosions of poetry, song, dance, tenderness, and love. The harshest sacrifices are linked with celebration. The problem arises when we come to "theological reflection," and we have to come to it. We begin to see Manichean dualism and juxtapositions. But the original experience is that women's struggle does not run parallel to the cause of the whole people; on the contrary, it is a structural part of total liberation.

You know that the team at DEI in San José is reflecting on the newness of the "specific struggles" on our continent within an overall utopian vision of a new society. These include the new presence on the continental scene of ethnic minorities, of women, and of blacks. I think the experience of the ethnic minorities might also happen to women. Among the ethnic minorities the class-ethnicity question has taken up a lot of our energy. The same can happen with regard to sex. Depending on where you place the emphasis, it can turn into a circular argument. To do theology from a women's perspective, for example, I wonder why we necessarily have to talk about women. *Women are more than themselves!* Of course they are economics and politics, but they are also nature, they have profound poetic and prophetic dimensions, they are "pregnant revolutions," and of course they are "revolutions in everyday life." We can speak of women as "the other half of the oppressed class," but on our continent we can also speak of women as "the other half of the theology of liberation."

Elsa: How do you perceive the reign of God from a women's perspective?

Raúl: To speak of God's reign is always difficult, for it is the impossible horizon that organizes our hopes for building possible societies. To consider how aware, organized, and mobilized women are anticipating God's reign, we have to situate their action within contemporary liberation movements, the central postulate of which is the affirmation of life. But we also have to remember that human beings have the capacity to anticipate an infinite variety of forms of life.

There are many forms and dimensions of the struggles to build new societies. I just want to refer to the so-called revolution of everyday life. As Agnes Heller has stressed, everyday life is a totality of activities comprising individual reproductions; these allow for the permanent possibility of social reproduction. That is, a sense of identity and belonging (and thus of difference) is based in primordial identities: notice how every nuclear family has its language and its symbols and almost a micro-world of myths. And the macro-world enters in, is engendered, and is perpetuated from generation to generation through, among other factors, everyday life. There is a socialization of vital experiences from infancy to old age that in daily practice maintain, consolidate, and at any given moment can cause ways of life and structures of value to become explosive. In the last analysis these experiences shape and define our "we," our collective consciousness, especially with regard to new societies.

It seems to me that when we try to do theology by resorting almost instinctively to "epic loci," we run the risk of losing this real dimension where multiple and qualitative elements of the new societies, that is, the anticipations of God's reign, are being built. The conception of ordinary, everyday life as fundamental helps us understand the Last Judgment in Matthew 25, where everything is related to everyday life. But not only in this passage; the Bible is full of everyday life experiences and wisdom in anecdotes, narratives, and other literary forms. But I'm convinced that it is here, in everyday reality, that we find one of the possibilities, both on the practical and theoretical levels, for the action and presence of women.

All of life is to be found basically in everyday life. And it is in these concrete expressions of life that we find anticipations of God's reign. Everyday life not only reproduces labor power for the dominant system. It also produces and reproduces life as resistance or as revolutionary reversal. It reproduces ethical and aesthetic values, forms of personal and social relationships, new expressions of the future that form part of this "intangible capital" of the people. And of course in this women play an essential role.

Before and after the date of the triumph of liberation, we find furrows on the map of everyday life. And women are half the seed that is sown there and will grow. This is my assurance and my hope, new earths and new heavens.

Mortimer Arias

San José, Costa Rica, August 1986

Mortimer lives a block and a half from my house, and he's the rector at the Seminario Bíblico Latinoamericano, where I teach. We agreed to meet at 7:00, after supper, in the apartment where he lives with his wife, Beatriz. His apartment is very warm, lovingly decorated. I had a cassette that was blank on one side, which I thought would be enough; but we needed another. Mortimer lent me one with classical music on it, which I used to finish the interview. As I was about to leave, Mortimer remembered something that he wanted to add, if it was okay with me. I told him of course, and so we plugged in the recorder again — and ate some more bread and salami. It was about 8 p.m.

Elsa: Mortimer, you consider women's oppression to be real. Tell me a little about your personal experience of it.

Mortimer: My experience is quite diverse. I was brought up in a small country, Uruguay. Just as Costa Rica likes to think of itself as the Switzerland of Central America, Uruguay is known as the Switzerland of South America. Uruguay has in fact been a noteworthy experiment in modernization, a country that made a great deal of progress in education and democratic organization in the creation of a welfare state. It became a model, one of the countries most advanced in social legislation. The

121

legislation included abundant, increasing, and constant components for the welfare of women — their working conditions, schedules, salaries, maternity leaves, education. I've experienced this since I was a child in a coeducational grammar school, in high school, and in the university, where women had equal opportunities with men. Together with Chile and some other countries, Uruguay was one of the first countries to recognize the civil and political rights of women.

So my experience during this first period was of a liberal, democratic society, which was attempting to improve social conditions, including those of women. But even within that society the oppression of women in the family and society in general was obvious on the level of images and male chauvinist stereotypes. Our creole society inherited this machismo from Spain and reinforced it during the gestation of our "Gaucho" society.

A Bolivian anthropologist, Montaño, has done a very interesting study of machismo. He relates it to cultures where the horse is very important, showing how a certain type of machismo reinforces the image of the strong outdoorsman; women are expected to stay at home, cultivating "feminine" virtues. He shows that these equestrian cultures can be found among the Arabs, North American cowboys, the Gauchos of Río de la Plata, and in the eastern parts of Bolivia, where he writes.

Women's situation varies with the context. In Bolivia, for example, there are three forms of family organization with different racial components. There are the Indians, the mestizos, and the whites.

The whites are descendants of the Spaniards in the Santa Cruz and Beni areas, the cattle-raising zones of the eastern plains of Bolivia, which are quite similar to the plains of Argentina and Uruguay in their Spanish component and equestrian culture.

In mestizo society the *cholo** woman, is a kind of matriarch. In Cochabamba and La Paz, *cholo* women control the entire

---

* *Cholo, chola,* of mixed white and Indian ancestry.

commercial network that extends throughout the country and beyond. The urbanized *cholas* are persons with great power. Men are secondary, insignificant. They appear only at the moment of conception or at the fiestas or as servants. The *cholo* market women control the porters, who are Indian men. And they are the owners of fleets of trucks that make up the distribution network of the country. They often travel in the trucks alongside their husbands, who are the drivers. They are women with children, but they are in control, they are the center.

The Indian family in the rural areas of Bolivia is a work unit. It is a traditional society where men, women, and children all work together on the same plot of ground and divide up the tasks. Women work on the land like the men, but the men do the weaving while the women do the spinning.

Elsa: And the decision making?

Mortimer: I'm not familiar enough with the internal workings of indigenous culture to say. I know men have the decision-making power on a community level. When the elders or community leaders meet, the women are separate.

This has been an excursus, a parenthesis, in our discussion of the three forms of family organization and man-woman roles in Bolivia. What Montaño says can be applied to the equestrian culture that we find in the highly developed zone of eastern Bolivia. This is the cultural pattern in which I was raised. It was very male chauvinist and...

Elsa: You say "very male chauvinist," but when you spoke of the active participation of the *cholas* was that male chauvinist?

Mortimer: I'm speaking now of Uruguay, not Bolivia. That's why I wanted to make it clear at the beginning that my background is in Uruguay, in a secularized society in a dizzying process of social, political, and democratic progress with very advanced social legislation, including educational opportunities for women. But on cultural and familial levels the male chauvinist patterns were of course maintained. Men were the head of the families. Masculine and feminine roles were especially stressed, and we were trained to be proud of being the male.

It is a tango culture where there are the two extremes of the reviled woman who is also adored. The tangos often depict "fallen" women, the woman who has run off with another man, who has abandoned him, who didn't appreciate his affection, and so forth, the evil woman. On the other hand, we find the veneration of the mother and the adoration of the beloved woman. This has been part of my background, and I have a very real strain of romanticism, an attitude of admiration and adoration toward women, but this is also an idealization of women.

A more immediate experience of the oppression of women occurs on a family level. There is an internalization of the role of woman as the mistress of the house, the cult of the sacrificing mother, and the notion of *"labores de su sexo,"* the "labors of her sex," as they still put on passports and identity cards, referring to housework and other tasks presumably proper to women. I have experienced this in a conscious way in my own home, and I have tried to compensate by helping with the household chores and taking on a helping role at critical times. For example, when my wife was sick in bed for long periods of time, I took care of the children and did the other jobs if we couldn't get outside help.

But my wife was always principally responsible for most of the housework, cleaning, cooking, laundry, and raising the children. So in a marriage like ours, with true partnership and mutual support and no explicit male chauvinist demands, my wife nevertheless had to sacrifice her career, her very clear vocation to work in Christian education. And this was because of the way family and society are organized.

Elsa: Mortimer, as a theologian you've written quite a bit on *el reino de Dios,* the reign of God. How would you reflect on the reign of God from a women's perspective?

Mortimer: That's something we have to ask the women theologians, like the one who is asking the questions here. I'm not able to speak from a women's perspective, but I think I can mention some implications. First of all, some women who are challenging the patriarchal tradition have difficulty with the term itself. *"Reino de Dios"* is a patriarchal term, in other languages even more than in Spanish. "Kingdom of God" in English is horrible; "kingdom" is the area belonging to the king. There is no "queen-dom." *"Reino"* in Spanish is a little more neutral and includes both men and women. (Sexist language in English is much more obvious than in Spanish.) Feminist theologians tell us that concepts having to do with reigns are a part of our patriarchal tradition, which includes a concept of God as father and king.

I have tried to confront this difficulty in my writing on God's reign, which is a theme stressed by Jesus; it is his original message. Any translation or interpretative term that we use doesn't express what the technical term in the Gospels means by reign, or rule, of God.* "Rule of God" might be the more appropriate term, for we're not referring to a territory, a jurisdiction, but to the action of God in the world, in history. So from a women's point of view there might be a certain resistance to the terms themselves.

On the other hand, when we explore the theme itself and the content and meaning that Jesus gave it, any suspicion of discrimination, hierarchism, or stratification vanishes. We see this not only in Jesus' parables, but in his attitudes and in his proclamation of God's reign. Some of Jesus' most important acts in announcing the reign that has come, is coming, and will come have to do with women. And this was one of the things that society couldn't accept — together with his attitude toward the marginalized, the poor, those suffering discrimination. He sought to rehabilitate women, to defend them, even to praise them.

In the case of the woman at Bethany, for example, who anointed Jesus' feet, Jesus truly makes of her a living text on the

---

* *Reino,* or *reinado, de Dios.*

meaning of the reign of God and the response to the presence
of the reign of God in terms of gratitude and love.

Elsa: Mortimer, it seems to me that in Latin America we often jump quite quickly from the reign of God, or the rule of
God, to "new society," without giving much importance to personal relationships. We collectivize society without dealing with
individual interrelationships, at least in an explicit way. Speaking from a women's perspective, it seems to me that when we
speak of the reign of God we need to keep very much in mind
the categories "new man" and "new woman" so that we take
into account the interpersonal relationships within the collec-
tivity that makes up the new society. Those actively working
for the coming of God's reign will then realize that there are relationships not only with the poor, but also with women, blacks,
indigenous people, children. What do you think?

Mortimer: I'm not sure I understand what you mean, because
in God's reign, as I understand Jesus' proclamation, there are
two levels: the personal and the communal, and there is a strategy of God's reign that includes both. We can see this, for
example, in the way Jesus called the disciples. It was a personal
call, a challenge. And when he announced God's reign to different persons who represented different sectors of society, for
example, Zaccheus or the rich young man, it was an eminently
personal call, but in the context of the community.

These two cases are very interesting. Jesus says to the rich
young man, very well, but now if you want to be perfect, if you
want to enter into God's reign, into life, which is the synonymous
term that Jesus uses, "sell what you have and give it to the
poor." This cannot be done without others, especially without
the poor. But the call is personal and the relationship that is
hoped for is personal.

The same occurs with Zaccheus. When Zaccheus makes his
option for the future, which is to return what he has unjustly
taken from society and from then on to give half his goods to the
poor, Jesus says to him, " 'Salvation' has come," that is, God's

reign has truly arrived. (Jesus more frequently uses the term "reign"; only rarely does he say "salvation.") There is a new relationship with the neighbor that involves economic realities, justice. Jesus deals with women in the same way.

Elsa: Let's talk some about the church, or do you want to say something else about the reign of God?

Mortimer: That's okay, whatever you like.

Elsa: You have been a pastor and a bishop. Tell me, in your experience what is women's position in the church and what do you see for the future?

Mortimer: I can speak of the Methodist church, which I know and to which I belong, where women have had considerable space, but only in certain areas. The case of the societies that women had to create because they did not have leadership roles in the church is well known. Now that I know the history of Methodism in the United States before it came to Latin America I realize what a long struggle it was for women to achieve the place that they now have. It was like the struggle of the blacks; first it was the blacks' struggle against slavery, and then against discrimination. We had the struggle of the laity in general in our episcopal structure with its strong authoritarian tendencies. It was a struggle that took time and various Methodist denominations emerged, for example, the Primitive Methodist church, the Free Methodist church, the Republican Methodist church. These represented forms of protest against the lack of lay representation and against the vertical authoritarianism of the bishop. The same thing happened with women, who were the last group to have a path opened within the Methodist church. Happily the Methodist church has shown itself quite capable of responding to new challenges and situations.

There was a very interesting case around 1918. For the first time five women were elected as delegates to the General Conference of the Methodist church in the United States. Among them was a great theologian, Georgia Harkness, who was very well respected by her academic peers. Nevertheless the church didn't have legislation that permitted women to be delegates to the General Conference. Some even used the roundabout argument that the Spanish word *"laico"* in English is "layman." It's lay*man,* they argued, and not lay*woman.* And she wasn't admitted as a delegate to the conference! It took eight years to change that legislation.

In Latin America there was space within the women's societies, and there were deaconesses as well. The woman I married was my classmate in the School of Theology in Buenos Aires. She studied theology, with specializations in Christian education as well as nursing, to work as a deaconess in the church. But the requirements of her work were such that she really functioned as the pastor of a local congregation, doing the same things that I was doing in Montevideo. At that time deaconesses couldn't be pastors. They had auxiliary tasks in social work, education, women's issues. She was an excellent pastor, better than I, but she couldn't be ordained.

When we got married, she had to give up her work as a deaconess, because deaconesses had to remain single. So she could no longer be a deaconess or receive a church salary, because she had married a pastor. During my entire pastorate she was a decisive factor, performing basic tasks within the church. But she was very restricted because she was the wife of a pastor, and that imposed certain expectations on her. This has been transcended, thank God, in the Methodist church, and for many years now women have been able to be pastors.

Elsa: Let's speak for a moment about the Bible, about hermeneutics. Do you think women are able to re-read the Bible from a women's perspective, considering that it's a book written in a patriarchal culture that contains many male chauvinist elements? Have you thought of some hermeneutical guidelines?

Mortimer: Not only do I think such a re-reading is possible, but I've already taken advantage of it. The most stimulating reading in hermeneutics recently has been that of feminist hermeneutics, starting with the book I have here, *La biblia de los oprimidos.** Although the book is not specifically feminist, it's very interesting and promising that in your analysis of the biblical terms for oppression you speak of the violation of women as one of the forms of oppression described in the Bible with great crudeness and power. Only a woman could call our attention to this dimension. I don't know if Thomas Hanks dealt with this or if it was you who discovered it.

Elsa: I elaborated it.

Mortimer: When I read this compendium on the language of oppression in Scripture, I was very impressed by the fact that this kind of oppression, the invasion of the body, the violation of a woman's integrity, can easily be missed by traditional hermeneutics. Later I had the privilege of reading your work on the Song of Songs, a truly fascinating reading, precisely because it brings out all the potential richness of the love poem. It is exegesis by one woman of what another woman felt and expressed in the Song, for it seems possible that at least parts of the Canticle were written by a woman; this has not always been thought of as a possibility.

I'm also learning a lot from the feminist exegetes and theologians in the United States: Letty Russell, Sheila Collins, Rosemary Ruether, Phyllis Trible, and Phyllis Bird, who was my colleague and personal friend during the two years I spent at Perkins School of Theology in Dallas. I've also been reading Elisabeth Schüssler-Fiorenza, and this has been something of a revelation. Now, as you know, I cannot deal exegetically with a passage of Scripture without asking about the women's story submerged in the passage. You saw this today in our treatment of the Last Supper and the question of who got the most important seat, or in our interpretation of the Resurrection story.[†]

---

*Elsa Tamez, *La biblia de los oprimidos* (San José, Costa Rica: DEI, 1979); Eng. trans.: *The Bible of the Oppressed* (Orbis Books, 1982).

[†]Mortimer is referring to a sermon he had preached that morning in the chapel of the Seminario Bíblico Latinoamericano.

In conclusion I want to say that I consider it a great privilege to live in this time when new dimensions of liberation are being discovered, particularly this dimension that comes from women. I'm very grateful to be continuously re-educated by women, whether my closest companion, my friends in the ministry, my colleagues in the seminary, or the theologians or exegetes whom I read and from whom I learn. I especially want to mention how tremendously enriching it has been in recent months to share my life with a woman who has had her own career as a Christian worker.* We can live and work together in a common project, without having to tie ourselves down to customary expectations and roles in the home. In all this I feel that women are contributing to human liberation. I am speaking too of the liberation of men.

Elsa: Thank you very much, Mortimer.

---

*Mortimer married a second time after the death of his first wife.

Part II

COMMENTARY

THERE IS A WONDERFUL RICHNESS to these interviews, a richness that stems precisely from the interview genre, which allows for spontaneity. There was not time for the reflection necessary to polish the expressions and buttress them with footnotes. Citations were replaced by "Doña Antonieta," "my wife," "the lady who took care of me..." — that is, the voice of the school of life. The words depict for us reality as the theologians see it, and at the same time they become a mirror useful for self-criticism. This is one of the great values of the book: we can initiate the dialogue at more personal and honest levels, at levels efficacious in everyday life.

Here I dare to hold up certain points that, by my way of seeing, are important and arise from the interviews themselves. I say "dare" because I do not have behind me an organized feminist struggle that would provide solid foundation, nor studies in psychology that might verify some of the assertions that I will make. My ideas revolve around suspicions that come to me from personal experience and from other women. And so I follow the drift of the dialogue, thinking, as it were, out loud. Allow me, for now, to leave aside feminist theory on mercantile relationships of the capitalist system to speak in more personal terms.

There are many fruitful dimensions worthy of treatment, but it is not possible to cover them all. So I will comment on several of the four axes that we find in this book: reality, the church, theology, and hermeneutics. I should make it clear that my reflections are addressed to theologians who share the perspective of those who have opted for the oppressed. I presuppose certain criteria of the Latin American women's struggle, for example, the relationship of our struggle with the broader liberation movement.

The Reality: Easier Said Than Done

Is the oppression of women "real"? This is the question that
opens the dialogue. It is a simple, perhaps banal, question, but
its purpose is to surprise and to force us to situate ourselves
in the concrete space of our everyday existence. That is where
hearts must take a stand: they open or close. It is the moment
of self-criticism or self-deception.

Women are not exempt from the question; we live it — but
from a deeper angle and one step ahead. For every step that
a woman takes against her oppression, there is a corresponding
step of resistance, whether silent or violent. Rarely are the paces
the same. The journey is painful and it causes women to walk
more slowly or, in some cases, to become immobilized.

When asked about oppression the men, if they are sincere,
must recognize its reality. But they also feel that they must
admit blame, acknowledge their privileged status. They feel
bad and often become needlessly defensive, like the way whites
often react to blacks. And so the women's issue in the popular
movement is highly and secretly polemical. It is painful to air
it because we all are affected by it very personally. We are all
either male or female, a polarity that is not present between rich
and poor.

We are facing an impasse that we must overcome. It is indeed extremely important that men pass through this first stage
of accepting a reality that is unjust to women under our present
system, a reality that favors men, and that men with their daily
behavior reinforce. This is pure and simple honesty. But we
must take the next step, namely, What should we do about
this reality? I suspect that taking this step will diminish the
fear of confronting the issue. It is not that women depend on
men; the fulfillment of women as persons of dignity can occur
without men, but that would create an unhappy society, full of
bitterness, resentment, and frustration. For men and women
were created to live together and to love each other, to re-create
the world in harmony. And this cannot happen when men domi-

nate women, or when women are liberated separately from men. And this is not a question of individual cases ("I know a woman who...". Rather it is a process that tends to forge a new way of being women and of being men, protagonists of a new world.

But the leap to everyday life is extremely difficult. The theologians recognize this when they say that it is one thing to say it and another thing to do it. The question led them to think about their own situations in relation to women and prompted them to an awareness of their privileged situation (Míguez Bonino, Pixley, Gutiérrez, de Santa Ana). And the common space of the male is comfortably distant from everyday life in the private sphere. Women take care of the dishes, the meals, the clothes, the floors, the waiting in the doctor's office with the children, shopping, that is, the things that *have to be done,* that somebody has to do, and that somebody is almost "naturally" the woman, according to the criteria of macho ideology. The men let themselves be seduced by the agreeable culture of Latin America. I think if I were a man I would be ensnared by this magic too: I would not do what I would want to do, and what I would do I would not want to do. But these cultural mechanisms are so solidly and subtly constructed that if we intend to try to transform this unjust reality we swim against a very strong current.

We must transform the man-woman relationship in everyday life, and men should include this relationship within all their disappointment and fatigue: this is the daily struggle. This struggle has always been "natural" for poor women, for indigenous women, for black women, for *mestizo* women, for peasant women, for working women, for middle-class women. For there is a truth here that we cannot overlook and that we who seek a new order of life must embrace: the foretastes of utopia are experienced in everyday life, and it is in everyday life that we begin to build this utopia (Vidales). There is no place else. And everyday life in the private sphere is the focal point for re-establishing a new relationship that will have its effect in the public sphere.

If all this is true, then the basic question is how do we do it, how can we make this leap to daily life. It is not up to me to deal with this here, nor is it up to any one person; rather this needs to be a collective discussion with a profound openness, dialogue, concrete action. Nonetheless I believe that within this process the challenge to overcome our fears and to face the issues of women — and this is true for both men and women — must be dealt with very seriously. This is mentioned by Frei Betto, Julio de Santa Ana, Hugo Assmann, and others. So we must begin by clarifying whether or not such fears do indeed exist, why they do, what the fear is of, and how to overcome it. I think that this is an important step toward everyday life in the private sphere, which, of course, is always present in the public sphere.

Finally I want to emphasize a point mentioned especially by Gustavo Gutiérrez and Pablo Richard, namely, that when women are discriminated against all of society loses. Gustavo speaks of the repercussions of the marginalization of women. This, he says, makes for "a sick human society," and later he adds, "I think that we need to join in solidarity with women's demands because otherwise we miss out on too much ourselves." And Pablo Richard says, "Women are the principal victims of the oppression, but they aren't the only ones. All of reality in all its dimensions is affected by the oppression of women." Richard emphasizes the close relationship between the overall reality and the special situation of the feminine sector and how they mutually affect each other both positively and negatively. It is very promising to see that nearly all the theologians mention something along these lines in their interviews, for example, Mesters, Boff, Míguez Bonino, as they theologize from a women's perspective. And this, I believe, is an attitude that will help both men and women in the process of women's liberation, which, as we have said, involves the liberation of both sexes.

The Church: A Sin in History

We find a certain difference between the Protestant and Catholic theologians with regard to women and the church. The Catholic theologians speak of the obvious marginalization of women in the church. Boff considers it "a historical sin." All of them acknowledge the exclusive control of men in administration and governance, with no theological or biblical justification. Nonetheless all of them happily mention the central role of women in the basic Christian communities. Because of its communitarian structure this new model of the Latin American church allows for a significant participation of women, which is not to be found in the official institutional model. The Protestant theologians speak of ever greater advances with regard to women's participation in ministry, especially ordination. But they also recognize that women are still second-class citizens — a term used by both Protestants and Catholics — to a greater or lesser degree depending on the denomination. The prevailing model of the pastor is a masculine one, and ordained women use that model. On the other hand, people cannot accept a woman in a pastoral role, and they are not used to seeing a woman with episcopal functions. Protestant and Catholic theologians agree that there are more women than men in the church and that women have always been more active in the activities of the church. But usually their responsibilities have been secondary ones.

The differences among the theologians are due to the different traditions and types of organization of their churches. What is most promising in this regard is that in Latin America we are seeing another model of church, the church born of the people. Within the space of that church women are finding a place where they can fulfill themselves and make great contributions. Although the phenomenon of the basic Christian communities is seen especially in Catholic sectors, it is not coincidental that in some Protestant churches that have taken a stand for human rights and the rights of the marginalized, women are making their presence felt on leadership levels in an unprecedented way. This is the case in the Methodist church in Argentina and Brazil.

The qualitative participation of women in the popular Christian communities is becoming a challenge to the institutional church. And as the participation of women increases, the antifeminist attitude of the churches will become less and less viable. Especially important in this regard is the role of women religious — the army of the ecclesial infrastructure, according to Dussel's notion.

But all this we know, and we have spoken of it on numerous occasions. It might be important here to consider more profoundly the woman/church question. The question is a delicate one, especially in the Catholic church, but not only there. In the Presbyterian church of Mexico, for example, the ordination of women is taboo.

I do not have the credentials to provide a definitive treatment of the theme, for I am not a pastor, nor do I belong to the Catholic church, which with its official face presents such an extreme example of the marginalization of women. But I think it is worthwhile to sketch out certain burning issues.

The first question that comes to mind is why should the issue of women be so sensitive in the church. What is the obstacle that prevents our fully facing up to the question? We know that there are no biblical or theological reasons preventing the participation of women at the same level as men. Nor is there any such obstacle in the documents of church tradition, as Dussel points out. What, then, is the cause of the fear? In the secular world there has been progress in the acceptance of women on leadership levels. In biblical and theological studies women have also been making progress; there are women professors of theology. Then why are women discriminated against in the official church and why is the question so sensitive? As we have said the issue is everywhere polemical, even in the popular movements. The difference is that in these movements there is a very clear and important presence of women; the sensitive questions are found more at a personal level in the private sphere. But, it seems to me, in the institutional church women do not have even a minimal significant space.

I know and I believe that this is not the banner to be raised by Latin American theology at this moment, nor is there much interest in the question among the women of the basic communities. Rather, as Gutiérrez says, these women have purely and simply taken for themselves this space within the church. Nonetheless, I think it can help us to understand discrimination against women if we ask this kind of question. Lately I have been thinking that the woman/church theme is so central because it deals with concrete issues and points to the total restructuring of the church. To do theology from a women's perspective is not dangerous, at least in the first instance, nor is a feminist re-reading of the Bible. But to discuss the question of women and the church is dangerous, because it touches on a concrete reality and requires visible actions. Perhaps this is why the issue is so sensitive: it touches on structure, and particularly the power structure.

Though it might seem absurd, I have the intuition that celibacy has something to do with this. It unintentionally fosters both machismo and verticalism. On the one hand it reinforces the unconscious fear of women, who have always been blamed for the "fall of man," a threat to the priesthood. For generally women have been seen more for their sex than for their ability to dialogue as persons. On the other hand celibacy enables those in leadership positions to have greater control over those in lower positions, for no one — particularly family members — stands in the way of church leaders utilizing priests or religious. One of the problems in the vertical structures of the episcopally organized Protestant churches is precisely the married pastor, whose transfer often causes family difficulties.

We can engage in positive reinterpretations of celibacy, as enabling a greater commitment to the poor. (I can affirm this notion from my own experience as a married woman with children.) But it is difficult to deny the negative effects celibacy has had. And I am happy to see that Frei Betto, Hugo Assmann,

Rubem Alves, and others have mentioned the theme of sensuality, pleasure, and the positive approach to the body, for they thereby help to demythologize sex. I am basing my suspicions on my experience as a woman in the Protestant church and on dialogues with Catholic women theologians and religious. It will be up to the Catholic women to do the necessary in-depth work on the subject.

A final point that I want to mention is the problem with regard to ordination faced by women among the people themselves. In many Protestant churches women still experience a rejection by the congregation, even by women. The problem will be all the more serious in the Catholic church, where the issue has not even been raised openly in Latin America. It seems that there has been a divinization of the masculine. Women have been oppressed by symbolic goods, for they have not had access to their production. The faithful are accustomed to see men on the altar performing the sacred liturgical functions. This gives the impression that masculinity has become sacred in this centuries-old custom. For this reason any change in the priestly ministry is difficult; an entire re-education of the Christian people is required.

Notwithstanding this challenge that we will one day have to confront, we want to emphasize and encourage the great opening that exists for women in the basic Christian communities, a truly epoch-making phenomenon that will be the point of departure for the renewal of the official institutional church. On this we agree with Pablo Richard when he says that women play an extremely important role in the change of models of the church: from a Christendom model to the church born of the people.

Theology: Something New Here and There

Carlos Mesters concludes his interview with the words, "Here and there something new is happening." And he is correct, for in Latin America we are passing through a moment of blessing in the sense that everything — reality, church, Bible, theology, human relationships — has become new. We are in a time of reinterpretation, of re-reading the signs of the times, of a search for new meanings, in sum, of transformation. And women, both as subjects and a theme, have emerged very quickly in recent years.

In the theological arena, the theology of liberation has been crucial for the incorporation of women into the theological task. In the words of Brazilian theologian Maria Clara Bingemer: "For me personally, as a woman, the theology of liberation has been most valuable, even in helping me to understand my own possibility of doing theology." To do theology from a woman's perspective outside the framework of the theology of liberation leads nowhere.

Therefore women with a theological vocation consider ourselves to be part of the Latin American theology of liberation and therefore too we believe that it is our responsibility to provide an explicit feminine presence and to promote the women's struggle within this theology. We are few in number but we are growing, and we are making ourselves felt in the world of theology, in spite of the many lacunae that still exist. The interviews are living testimony to this as demonstrated in the sincerity and good will of the theologians. The effort that they are making to recreate theology from a woman's perspective has inestimable value.

José Míguez Bonino, Leonardo Boff, Mortimer Arias, and others are attempting to incorporate new perspectives into their theology, and they have come up with some surprising results. One of the great merits of these interviews is precisely that they have encouraged these theologians to discover other dimensions to the theological task. This clearly does not mean that they will now teach us to do theology from a women's perspective. They understand this very well, for all of them have been very careful to say that the task is not theirs. Their intention is clear: it is important to begin to think from a women's perspective and simultaneously to break out of rationalistic discourse considered as the only valid and perfect way of knowing. One of the ways

to break out of this discourse is to try new approaches on the
basis of the feminine dimension.

This leads us to consider the question of feminine contributions. Is there such a thing? In most, if not all, of the interviews,
and in the questions as well, a special, though not exclusive,
contribution of women is presupposed. The nature of this contribution is not entirely clear, but everyone perceives it, and in
some we find certain striking constants.

To speak of the special contribution of women presupposes
that women have a particular identity. But unfortunately we are
not very clear about this specific identity. We note certain tendencies, but we do not know if they come from the cultural environment or from women's biological nature. It is clear enough
that men and women are not the same. Julio de Santa Ana
asserts that "the perception or the experience of God is not the
same for women as for men. I have no doubt about this. Nor is
the experience of Jesus Christ or the Holy Spirit or the church."
If this is the case, women will have a profound effect on theology, for as Gustavo Gutiérrez says, theological methodology
and spirituality are intimately related.

With regard to differences, I think that we must probe beneath certain qualities that are outstanding in women, like tenderness, which seems to be more common in women and has
therefore been undervalued. It seems that women have a different way of conceiving reality. Míguez Bonino, Vidales, Betto,
Richard, Boff, Schwantes, and others are not mistaken when
they assert that women are closer to concrete realities, to vital processes, and that their vision is more comprehensive and
unifying, that they operate more with categories of relationship than of distinction. Therefore they are able more easily
to break out of the eminently masculine dualism common to
Western thought.

This does not mean that women are not capable of decod-
ing reality in an analytical way, but that their grasp of reality
is in the first instance comprehensive and unifying. If this is
the case, the contribution to theology of a feminine perspective

is truly rich, as Míguez Bonino points out in his reflection on justification by faith. If this human perspective with a feminist tendency is taken seriously and promoted in all human beings, I believe that it will contribute to the liberation of theological discourse as well as of male theologians. Women will no longer be considered an "enigma," as some would have it, but rather as persons who grasp a more complex vision of the world and whose actions therefore respond to a different way of relating; they will thereby enrich both culture and theology.

We know that we are at the very beginnings of this process and that there is much to be done. But seeing "something new here and there" encourages us to continue the journey.

What does it mean to be a man? It is up to the men to address this question. Dussel has begun the process.

The Bible: Hermeneutical Audacity

Among the new things emerging here and there, hermeneutics from a women's perspective holds a special place. Women have had to confront countless biblical readings that discriminate against women, which, we can say, they have been able to "unpack." They have also had to confront the Bible itself, a book written in a patriarchal culture that therefore reflects masculine interests to the detriment of feminine ones. And finally, as a consequence, they have had to broach subjects that are sensitive from the point of view of orthodoxy, like the doctrine of biblical authority. I believe that this is the reason for their acknowledged creativity in the reading of the Bible. It is significant that Assmann says that in thirty or forty years we will see the Bible in a different way thanks especially to the hermeneutics of women.

This hermeneutical struggle has been very important for the struggle of Christian women. For who can deny that the Sacred Scripture has been and continues to be utilized as the basis for the marginalization of women? The hermeneutical question is sensitive and complex, because it involves the entire traditional concept of the sacralization of a patriarchal culture. And depending on the way we approach the Bible, the macho attitudes of our culture today are strengthened or undermined. At least this is what has happened, especially in Protestant circles.

With regard to the struggle against macho readings of the Bible, it seems to me that we have made much progress. Women of the church are increasingly suspicious of interpretations made outside the context of the text and prefer to look at the texts themselves. They reject what others say the text says. This is very common in the Catholic and Protestant basic communities. Mesters and Schwantes cite examples.

Confrontation with the Bible itself is more complicated. Criteria of discernment are required to separate revelation from the interests of Hebrew males. In this regard the dialogues with Juan Luis Segundo and Jorge Pixley are very fruitful. Juan Luis reinterprets, or rather enriches, his hermeneutic circle by applying ideological suspicion not only to the reality from which we begin but to the text itself. This is unquestionably hermeneutical audacity, at least from a fundamentalist point of view. But from the point of view of faithfulness to Christ it is in fact a search for the meaning of the gospel. If women dare to question the text itself it is because we believe that God has created women in the divine image and likeness and that any sexist discrimination tarnishes this divine image in women.

Women must recognize, then, that there are texts in the Bible that reflect an attitude contrary to the gospel itself and are rooted in a particular culture. There are texts that are impossible to re-read from a liberating perspective, and, as Pixley points out, cannot be normative. We are not imposing our own criteria on the text; rather, the Bible itself, considered as a whole, paradoxically provides the criteria. God in favor of the oppressed is the Latin American feminist hermeneutical key. This key is seen very clearly in the axes proposed by Jorge (the Exodus and Jesus), but it runs through the whole Bible. And it seems to me that this criterion is more than the well-known notion of the canon within the canon. The faith in which God continues to be revealed today through the Holy Spirit inspires these hermeneutical approaches.

According to Juan Luis, suspicion in the text is easy to see. Strangely enough, exegetes have missed it for a long time. Only now have women (especially First World women) infiltrated what had been a masculine discipline and made brilliant contributions. These are not reducible to a reinterpretation of women in the texts but rather have enriched exegetical and hermeneutical methodology in general.

Juan Luis points out a very important dimension of the hermeneutical process when he says that one of the questions we should ask of the text is: "What did women of that time think?" This question proceeds from his previous step of purifying the message of a masculine influence; he asks, "If I eliminate from this message the aspects that derive from male domination of women, what do I have to put back?" The answer to this question is provided by the previous question of what the women of that time thought. Although it seems quite simple, this question, I think, is one of the steps we must take for the reconstruction of the text. And here lies its importance, for it suggests the task we must undertake. So I do not think we need simply to "complement an exclusively male point of view," as Juan Luis says. It is more than this; it is to reconstruct history from the point of view of the absent women who have been deemed inferior. And this could very likely change a large part of that history.

We are searching for new hermeneutical guidelines from a women's perspective. Here we must note that those providing the elements for these guidelines are the women of the popular Christian communities who dare to read the Bible in a different way, and not only the passages that speak of women, but all the texts. In the experience of Milton Schwantes, there is a clear difference between the readings of women and of men, for the reading of women is more concrete, closer to daily life. As Milton says, "Women are able to be more in tune with the biblical testimony from the perspective of the poor." So there is much to learn from women. Pablo Richard believes that hermeneutics from a feminist perspective has helped him see things that he had not seen before.

This audacious approach of women to the Bible is leading to a reconsideration not only of the doctrine of biblical authority and the traditional hermeneutical process, but also of other aspects of biblical scholarship that have gone unquestioned. And here male biblical scholars can be of help. Milton suspects that a large part of the production of the Bible comes from a peasant culture within a tributary mode of production. He thinks that women played a major role and that therefore their voice was very much present in the production of the texts. I don't know about this, but if someone is suspicious, it would be worthwhile to begin to question all of biblical scholarship — leaving aside the presuppositions.

Finally I want to mention something related to inclusive language. Here we find a diversity of opinion among the theologians. It profoundly annoys Rubem Alves to speak of God as "he/she" at the same time, and he gives his reasons for his opinion. Pablo Richard looks with favor on the phrase "God is she...." Hermeneutically speaking it strikes Juan Luis Segundo as inconsistent to make God into a woman when Hebrew culture called God a man, and Gustavo Gutiérrez considers it extremely important to include women in language. The opinions have different nuances. In Rubem's case, for example, it is one thing to recognize sexist language, which he does, and another to assign to God two sexes at the same time. Gustavo says nothing about the name of God, and Juan Luis mentions nothing about exclusive everyday language, though I believe he would acknowledge that such language exists.

The truth is that the problem of exclusive language has not been vigorously addressed by women in Latin America. As I understand it, in the First World it is an almost obsessive battle. This is perhaps because in English the exclusion is more obvious than in Spanish, as Arias points out. But Spanish is discriminatory as well and reflects a view of the world and a grammatical structure centered on the male. This is a reality we must acknowledge; Latin American women do recognize it. Nonetheless in a process of liberation like ours in Latin America, this is but one of the aspects that in practice must be changed simultaneously with macho attitudes and behavior. For in the final analysis, such attitudes and behavior will determine the efficacy of our struggle. In concrete terms, the use of inclusive language does not necessarily imply acting on behalf of women. I am referring to the present stage of the struggle of Latin American women. But I do feel that language is very important. We must begin to appropriate it and to discover the degree of discrimination that women feel in language; this becomes especially apparent when women take an active role in the popular struggle. (At the time of the triumph of the Nicaraguan revolution, a TV report announced that the *niños* were the favorites of the revolution. A six-year-old niece of mine asked in confusion, "And the *niñas* too, right?")

The name we give to God is a question that still seems strange in our context. When theologians here speak about inclusive language with reference to God, they are not speaking within a Latin American framework. I am sure that they have in mind the discussion among First World feminists. Because in both Catholic and Protestant popular Christian communities it has occurred to no one to speak of Goddess, or to refer to the God of the Bible as mother. And generally speaking this is still alien to Latin American feminist Christian women, or at least we do not consider it an important issue — yet. Personally I find more interesting the suggestion of Dorothee Sölle to call God Water, Light, Path, Bread, Life....

The Journey Ahead

There is much yet to be done. We search out the path as we go. We discern the way, following some paths, rejecting others. Sometimes we learn by our mistakes. But the important thing is that now we know that there is a journey to be undertaken.

In a companion volume to this work Latin American women theologians will broaden and deepen the dialogue that I have barely begun here. The result will be very gratifying, for it will represent another step in the process of liberation. I guarantee it.

Contributors

Juan Luis Segundo: Uruguayan. Jesuit priest and theologian. Author of the five-volume *Theology for Artisans of a New Humanity* and *The Liberation of Theology*

Julio de Santa Ana: Uruguayan theologian, philosopher, and sociologist. Author of *Good News to the Poor: The Challenge of the Poor in the History of the Church.*

Jorge Pixley: North American, raised in Nicaragua. Ordained Baptist minister. Author of *God's Kingdom: A Guide for Biblical Study* and *On Exodus: A Liberation Perspective.*

Hugo Assmann: Brazilian theologian, social scientist, university professor. Author of *Theology for a Nomad Church.*

Gustavo Gutiérrez: Peruvian priest and professor of theology in Lima. Author of *A Theology of Liberation* and *We Drink from Our Own Wells.*

José Míguez Bonino: Ordained Methodist minister and professor of theology and ethics at ISEDET, Buenos Aires. Argentinean. Author of *Doing Theology in a Revolutionary Situation.*

Enrique Dussel: Catholic lay theologian, church historian, and ethicist. Argentinean. Author of *History and the Theology of Liberation.*

Rubem Alves: Brazilian theologian and social scientist. Professor at Campinas State University. Author of *Tomorrow's Child* and *What Is Religion?*

Carlos Mesters: Dutch missionary in Brazil. Carmelite priest and Scripture scholar. Author of many Scripture studies for basic Christian communities.

Milton Schwantes: Brazilian Lutheran Scripture scholar. Author of "Projeto de Deus na Bíblia," in *Fé e Educação Política*, and "Von unten gesehen: Die Bibel als Buch der Befreiung gelesen," in *Evangelische Kommentare*.

Frei Betto: Brazilian Dominican lay brother and theologian. Editor of *Fidel and Religion*.

Leonardo Boff: Brazilian Franciscan priest, theologian, and professor of theology. Author of *Jesus Christ Liberator* and *The Church: Charism and Power*.

Pablo Richard: Chilean Catholic church historian and Scripture scholar. Staff member of the Departamento Ecuménico de Investigaciones, San José, Costa Rica. Author of *The Death of Christendom, Birth of the Church*.

Raúl Vidales: Mexican theologian, social scientist, and grassroots organizer. Author of *Práctica religiosa y proyecto histórico* (with Tokihiro Kudó).

Mortimer Arias: Methodist bishop and theologian. Uruguayan. Rector of the Seminario Bíblico Latinoamericano, San José, Costa Rica. Author of *Announcing the Reign of God: Evangelization and the Subversive Memory of Jesus*.